DECORATING WITH
TRADITIONAL
FABRICS

Miranda Innes

DECORATING WITH TRADITIONAL FABRICS

Simply made soft furnishings for today's home

BCA

LONDON   NEW YORK   SYDNEY   TORONTO

This edition published 1994 by BCA
by arrangement with Collins & Brown

First published in Great Britain in 1994
by Collins & Brown Limited

CN 6391

Conceived, edited and designed by Collins & Brown Limited

Editor **Colin Ziegler**
Art Director **Roger Bristow**
Designed by **Steven Wooster**
Photographer **Clive Streeter**
Stylist **Lucinda Egerton**

Filmset by Servis Filmsetting Ltd, Manchester
Reproduction by Daylight, Singapore
Printed and Bound in Italy by L. E. G. O., Vicenza

Contents

BEDDING

SEATING

CURTAINS

TABLECLOTHS AND BAGS

Introduction

NOTHING BEATS MAKING SOMETHING for a glow of satisfaction, and, of the whole repertoire of creative activity, sewing is the most rewarding and soothing of pastimes. In this book, there is a collection of projects which will take a few hours at most to make, require less skill than style, and which will still look good a decade from now. In other words, this is a book for today's homemaker who does not have the time to fathom the intricacies of upholstery and who wants to make something now that looks good immediately.

Textiles are one of the earliest creations of human artistry and ingenuity and they continue to be one of the great enrichments of life. Life without fabrics would be cold, harsh, and uncomfortable. In a futuristic nightmare of a scientist-designed ergonomically rationalized home, where there was no further need for textiles, I suspect that people would still find a way to smuggle them into their lives as there just is a part of human nature that craves their soft, warm allure.

Not only do textiles feel good in a way that nothing else can. They also look good. Every color under the sun is to be found in a fabric emporium. There are the natural fabrics – cotton, linen, silk, and shades of wool – whose subtle undyed colors need no adornment. There are natural dyes – indigo, madder, logwood, and onion skins for example – which impart soft colors with a magical, mutual affinity. These are colors that refuse to quarrel. After the advent of aniline dyes in Victorian times, no such claim could be made. Suddenly purple, turquoise, chrome yellow, and magenta could wreak havoc on the senses, and the legacy, much refined, of those heady experiments with color is still with us. Even the least artistic among us must feel a thrill at the sight of a sizzling spectrum of linen cloth in dahlia and chrysanthemum colors, or the classic seaside charms of indigo, sky blue chambray, and natural calico.

There are marriages of color that always work, and there are daring forays into the dramatic and new which

may succeed triumphantly straight off, or which may be induced to succeed with a calming touch of white, or a soothing addition of black. Like painting, using fabrics is not a hard and unchanging science. Mistakes can be modified, overwhelming kaleidoscopes of color can be lit differently, hung differently, given different companions, and suddenly they will work. The most important thing is to keep your courage about you, and to be guided by the quickening of your pulse. If scarlet, rose red, and black excite you, go for it. Ignore the gloom industry which will tell you that bright colors are only successful on the equator, and proclaim to the world that you like them.

Color is one aspect of fabric. Texture is another and has a huge bearing on the eventual look of a textile, the way it hangs and its light-reflecting qualities. Mercerized cotton has a smooth, polished staple that holds shape and color beautifully, whereas raw Indian cotton is fibrous and whiskery, and liable to lose its shape. Silk satin falls in sumptuous folds and drapes, whereas silk tweed can be as stiff and coarse as hessian. The soft draping qualities or crisp definition, the thinness or thickness, weight or airiness, the smooth or matt surface – these are all characteristics that should be weighed up and pondered.

In your search for fabrics, explore the markets at home. Pay a visit to antique and ethnic textile shops and galleries: a tiny piece of embroidery can become an evocative edging for a curtain, or a precious contrast on a cushion. And do not forget to keep your eyes open on your travels – look for the tiny luminous prints of Provence, coarse hand-blocked cotton and gossamer fine silk in India, brilliant stripes and embroidery in Central America.

Using fabrics is an art, not an unchanging science. There are no hard and fast rules. You may not get it right every time, but with experience you will gain an intuition for what works and what will not. Once you have overcome your initial *pudeur*, you will find that there is nothing so absorbing, rewarding, and relaxing after a hectic week, than sitting down with a pile of fabrics, a cup of tea and the manic gleam of creation in your eye.

Techniques

Measuring Up

With each project, we give precise measurements for how much fabric you need to buy. However, your final requirements will naturally vary according to personal needs. In this section, we give instructions for calculating how much fabric you need to make bedding, curtains, cushions, and tablecloths for your home.

Shrinkage Before buying furnishing fabric, it is important to check for shrinkage. Ask a store assistant whether your chosen fabric will shrink during laundering and, if necessary, buy additional fabric to allow for this – sometimes it is necessary to buy as much as one-third extra to allow for shrinkage. Always machine wash your fabric and lining to preshrink them before cutting and making up, just in case they shrink at different rates.

Colorfastness When buying furnishing fabric you should also check for colorfastness. This is especially important if you are combining different fabrics in one project – for example, if you are making a patchwork quilt. If possible, avoid buying non-colorfast fabrics. If you do decide to buy them, however, remember to dry clean your item to prevent the colors from running.

Patchwork If what you are making involves patchwork – such as with the Flying Geese Quilt or the Patchwork Wool Cushion – you must remember to allow extra fabric for all the seam allowances of the different pieces of fabric. As a general rule allow ⅜in (1cm) on the edges of each piece of fabric to be sewn together (see also specific projects).

BEDDING

Flat Sheets To estimate the length of fabric needed for a flat sheet, first measure from the head of the mattress to the foot of the mattress. Next, measure the mattress depth. The length of the sheet should equal the length plus twice the depth, plus 20in (50cm) tucking-under allowance, and 5in (12cm) for top and bottom hems. The width of fabric is calculated similarly. First measure from one side of the mattress to the other. Next, measure the mattress depth. The width of the sheet should equal the width plus twice the depth, plus 20in (50cm) tucking-under allowance, and 1½in (4cm) for hem allowances. For example, if you had a bed with a mattress 80in (203cm) long, 72in (183cm) wide, and 8in (20cm) deep, you would need a piece of fabric 121in (305cm) × 109½in (277cm).

Duvet Covers Duvets come in a variety of different sizes such as full size, 80 × 88in (200 × 220cm), and twin, 68 × 88in (170 × 220cm). For a duvet cover, you will need two pieces of fabric, each the length of your duvet plus ⅜in (1cm) for each seam allowance and 1⅜in (3.5cm) for the hems; and the width of your duvet plus ⅜in (1cm) for each side seam allowance. If the duvet cover has a facing, you will need another strip of fabric the width of your duvet, 4in (10cm) deep, plus ⅜in (1cm) for each seam allowance.

Quilts To estimate fabric for a quilt or coverlet, make up the bed with whatever will go under the quilt – like pillows and duvets – to arrive at the quilt's final dimensions. First, measure from the top of the bed down to the end, and add 10in (25cm) for the overhang and ⅜in (1cm) for each seam allowance. Next, measure the width of the bed and add 20in (50cm) for the overhang (10in [25cm] on either side) and ⅜in (1cm) for each seam allowance. 10in (25cm) gives a generous overhang, but you can vary this to your taste and to how high the bed is from the floor.

Pillowcases To calculate the fabric required for a plain pillowcase, start by measuring the length and width of your pillow. You will need a piece of fabric twice the pillow length plus 8in (20cm) for flap and seam allowances, and once the pillow width plus ⅜in (1cm) for each seam allowance.

CURTAINS AND BLINDS

Curtains The amount of fabric required for curtains depends on the window treatment you choose. Before measuring, it is important that you install all hardware – for example, tracks, rods, and runners – since the curtains should be made to fit the supporting device, not the window.

To calculate the finished length of your curtain (or curtains), measure from the top of the rod or track to the place where the hem will fall, either floor length or sill length. If you are making floor-length curtains, subtract ⅜in (1cm) from this measurement to allow the curtains to clear the floor. Next, add hem and heading allowances. Your heading allowance will vary according to the type of heading you choose (refer to manufacturer's instructions for individual requirements). Average hem allowances are 2in (5cm) for lightweight curtains and 3–6in (7.5–15cm) for heavier curtains, depending on their weight.

When estimating the finished width of your curtains, it is generally better to be generous rather than too exact. First measure the length of your rod or track, then multiply this measurement to give adequate fullness. If you are working with sheer or lightweight fabrics, multiply by three; for heavyweight fabrics, two, or, exceptionally, as little as one and a half times the finished width should suffice. To this width, add seam allowances (see each project for measurements), then divide the total by the width of your fabric. This will give the number of panels required.

Finally, to estimate the total length of fabric required, multiply the length of each curtain (including hem and heading allowances) by the total number of panels needed.

Lining will give your curtains a professional finish and will also help to keep out sunlight which might cause fading. When estimating lining requirements, always buy the same quantities as your chosen curtain material. If possible, buy lining fabric in the same width as your curtain fabric so seams match.

Cupboard Curtains These can be flat, gathered, or pleated, and your fabric requirements will depend on the style you choose and on the way the curtains are fitted. For fastening curtains with an elasticated rod, measure the length of the opening and add 5in (12.5cm) for seam allowances and channels for rods. Measure the width of the opening and multiply by two to three for gathered curtains and by three for pleated curtains. Add on 1in (2.5cm) for each side hem.

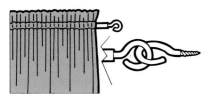

Use an elasticated rod (above) to hang cupboard curtains. Attach it to the cupboard with hooks and eyelets.

Tie-backs To establish the finished length of a tie-back, draw the curtain back as desired and measure around with a measuring tape, adding ⅜in (1cm) for each seam allowance. The width of the tie-back will vary according to the weight of your fabric – for example, narrow tie-backs suit sheer curtains, while heavy curtains require something wider. A guideline is 3–5in (8–13cm). The width of fabric you require is twice the finished width plus ⅜in (1cm) for each seam.

For plaited tie-backs (see p. 74), you need three strips of fabric, each 8in (20cm) wide, and the required length of your tie-back plus 6in (15cm) to allow for the shortening effect of the plaiting and wadding, and ⅜in (1cm) for each seam allowance.

Roller Blinds To determine the amount of fabric needed for a roller blind, first measure the width of your window recess. Deduct 1¼in (3cm) from this measurement to prevent the blind from catching in the brackets and add 2in (5cm) for hems. To estimate the length of fabric required for roller blinds, measure the drop from the top of the window recess to the window

sill. Add at least 1in (2.5cm) at the top to allow for securing the fabric to the roller, and 2¼in (5.75cm) at the bottom for hems (this can vary according to the width of your lath).

CUSHIONS

These vary considerably in size and shape, but for the purposes of this book we have concentrated on the square and rectangular knife-edge variety. For a cushion made from a single piece of fabric, you will need a piece twice the cushion length plus ⅜in (1cm) for each seam allowance, and the width plus ⅜in (1cm) for each seam allowance. If the cushion you are making has a different front and back, you need two pieces of fabric, each the length plus ⅜in (1cm) for each seam allowance, and the width plus ⅜in (1cm) for each seam allowance. You will need additional fabric depending on the type of closing employed. See individual projects for details.

TABLECLOTHS

Begin by measuring the length of your table top, through the middle, then measure the width. Now measure from the edge of the table top to the bottom of the required overhang; add ¾in (2cm) for hem allowances. The amount of fabric needed is the table length plus double the overhang, and hem allowances; and the table width plus double the overhang and hem allowances. If your tablecloth is for a dining table, the overhang should be at least 10in (25cm) clear of the ground. For example, if you had a table measuring 72in (183cm) × 36in (91cm), standing 30in (76cm) from the ground, you need a piece of fabric 112¾in (287cm) × 76¾in (195cm).

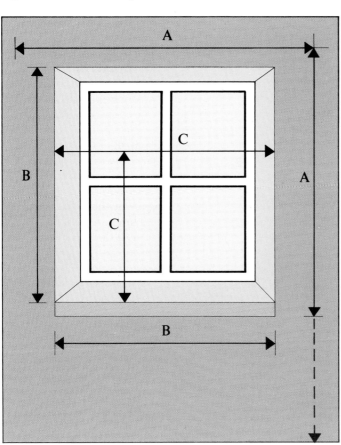

A×A: *measurements for wall-fixed curtains either sill or floor length.* B×B: *measurements for curtains or roller blinds inside the recess.* C×C: *measurements for café curtains.*

For occasional tables which are decorative rather than strictly functional, the tablecloth can be floor-length or even longer.

Preparing Your Cloth

Before you begin cutting, it is important to prepare your fabric carefully by straightening the ends of the cloth and pressing out creases. There are three methods of straightening the raw edges: tearing, drawing a thread, and cutting along a prominent pattern line, such as a stripe. While tearing is suitable for firmly woven fabrics, such as cotton lawn, it is unsuitable for knitted or loosely woven fabrics. To tear across the straight of grain, begin by snipping into one of the selvages using a pair of scissors. Next, grasp the fabric firmly with both hands and rip across to the opposite selvage to produce a straight edge. If your fabric is not suitable for tearing, you can draw out a thread and then cut along that line. First cut into the selvage, then gently pull the rip open to reveal the loose threads. Grasp one or two of the crosswise threads with your fingers and pull gently. The cloth will begin to gather up and, eventually, you will be able to pull out the entire thread. Now cut across the resulting straight line using a pair of scissors. Alternatively, let the pattern of the fabric be a guide for cutting.

Multiple Cutting If you are making something that requires a number of pieces of the same fabric all the same size, you can save time by cutting out several pieces at once. To do this, fold your fabric over and over until it is the maximum thickness you can cut through. Press the top layer of the fabric, making sure there are no wrinkles in the layers underneath, and pin all the layers together, checking that the edges line up. Mark the top layer of the fabric with the desired shape, pinning beside the marks to hold the fabric in place when cutting, and cut through all the layers at the same time. Be sure to fold and cut the fabric so that there is as little waste as possible. If the fabric you are using has a pattern or a stripe, be sure that the pattern or stripe is consistent on the different layers so that the cut pieces are all the same.

Cutting a Circle To cut a circle from a square piece of fabric, first fold the piece of fabric in half diagonally to form a triangle three times (see below). Press the fabric, making sure all the outer edges match up. Tie a piece of string around a tack and push the tack into the corner of the triangle that would be the center of the fabric if it were opened out (see bottom). Attach the other end of the piece of string to a pencil (as close to the point as possible) so that when the string is pulled taut, the distance from the tack to the pencil is the desired radius. With the pencil absolutely vertical, draw an arc. Pin the layers of fabric together outside this line and cut along it.

Mark diagonal

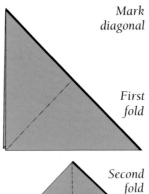

First fold

Second fold

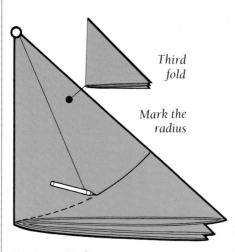

Third fold

Mark the radius

Cutting a Circle

Basic Stitches

Tacking Stitch Also known as a basting stitch, this is a temporary stitch used to hold together several layers of fabric during making up as a more secure alternative to pinning. The tacking stitch consists of a series of repeated straight stitches, each about ¼in (6mm) in length. You can tack with ordinary sewing thread, but it is best to use tacking thread, which is weaker than ordinary thread.

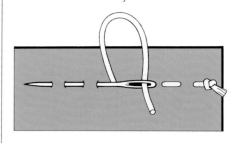

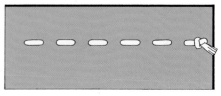

Basting Stitch

Blanket Stitch This is a decorative hand stitch which traditionally was used to finish the edges of thick woolen blankets, hence the name. Begin by turning under a hem on the wrong side. Next, secure the thread in the hem and insert the needle into the fabric from the right side about ⅜in (1cm) from the edge (**A**). Holding the working thread under the needle (**B**), pull through to create a loop. Repeat the process at ⅜in (1cm) intervals.

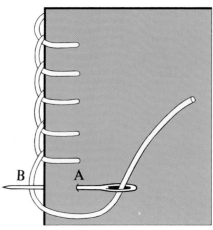

B   A

Blanket Stitch

Buttonhole Stitch Similar to the blanket stitch, the buttonhole stitch gives a firm, knotted edge that is ideal for neatening handworked buttonholes. With the edge of the fabric away from you, insert the needle upward through the fabric about ⅛in (3mm) from the raw edge. Twist the working thread around the tip of the needle, then pull the needle through to create a knot at the edge. Spacing can be large or small, depending on the purpose – for example, for hand buttonholes the stitches are made with no space in between. For machine-worked buttonholes, refer to your manufacturer's booklet.

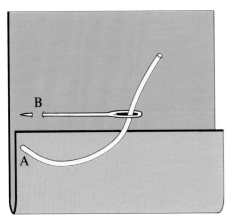

Buttonhole Stitch

Herringbone Stitch This stitch is ideal for hemming heavy fabrics, such as the door curtain on p. 70, because it enables you to neaten the raw edges as you sew. Stitches are worked from left to right, with the needle pointing left. First fasten the thread on the wrong side of the hem and bring the needle and thread through the hem edge (**A**). Take a very small stitch in the fabric directly above the hem edge and about ⅜in (1cm) to the right (**B**).

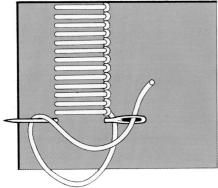

Herringbone Stitch

Take the next stitch ⅜in (1cm) to the right in the hem edge (**C**). Continue alternating stitches as illustrated.

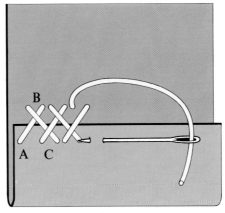

Herringbone Stitch

Slipstitch/Hemming Stitch This stitch is used when sewing a hem in place by hand. It is suitable for use on most fabrics and is ideal for use on lightweight fabrics. Working from right to left, fasten the thread and bring the needle out through the fold of the hem (**A**). Insert the needle into the main fabric and take a small stitch (**B**), taking care to catch only a few threads at a time so that the stitching will not show through on the right side. Opposite the first stitch, in the hem edge, insert the needle and slip it through the fold about ¼in (6mm) from the first stitch (**C**). Continue alternating stitches as illustrated.

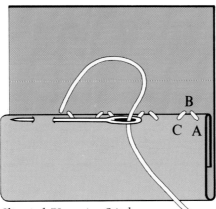

Slipstitch/Hemming Stitch

Stem Stitch This is a decorative stitch widely used for outlining letters and graphic images. Secure the thread on the wrong side and bring the needle through to the right side (**A**). Working from left to right, insert the needle back into the fabric (**B**) and bring it out

again half a stitch length between (**C**). Repeat the sequence, noting that C of the previous sequence becomes A in the next sequence.

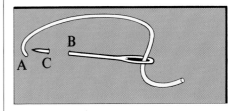

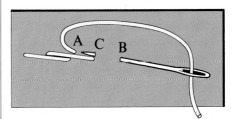

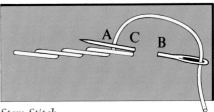

Stem Stitch

Reef Knot A reef knot (also called a square knot) is a secure method of tying cord. With a piece of cord in each hand, place the right cord (**A**) over the left (**B**) and bring the cord underneath (**1**). Now repeat the process, placing left cord over right (**2**). Pull tight (**3**).

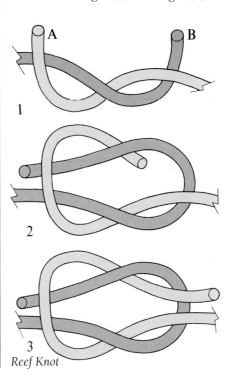

Reef Knot

11

Seams

Flat-fell Seam This is a sturdy seam ideal for items that need frequent laundering. It is used in making the Striped Patchwork Curtains on the wrong side of the fabric, but can be used on the right side as a decorative feature. With right sides together (if used on the wrong side), pin and stitch along the seamline, making sure that one seam allowance is ¼in (6mm) bigger than the other (**1**). Press the seam to one side so that the wider seam allowance covers the narrower one (**2**). Turn the edge of the wider seam allowance under the narrower one and press. Stitch this folded edge in position, close to the edge (**3**).

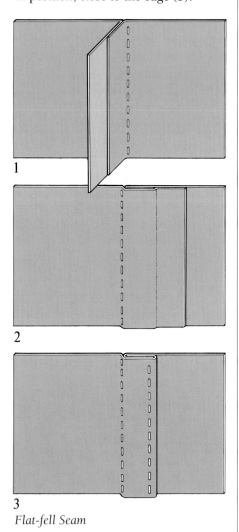

Flat-fell Seam

French Seam This seam is used mainly with lightweight fabrics to neaten and prevent fraying along straight edges. Pin the edges to be seamed wrong sides together and stitch ¼in (6mm) from raw edge (**1**). Turn, press, and pin right sides together; stitch ⅜in (1cm) away from previous seam (**2**) and turn right side out.

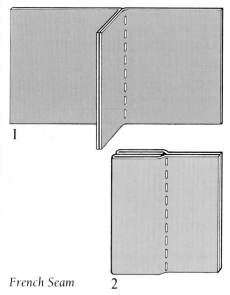

French Seam

Mitered Corners Corners can be neatly finished by mitering – the diagonal joining of two edges at a corner. First cut the border pieces to be joined at a 45° angle, leaving a ⅜in (1cm) seam allowance. Stitch the pieces together (see individual projects for whether right or wrong sides together), leaving ⅜in (1cm) unstitched at the inner ends (**1**). Pin and stitch the inner edges of the borders to the center panel all around (**2**) and press seams open. Trim the seams at the corners if they are too bulky.

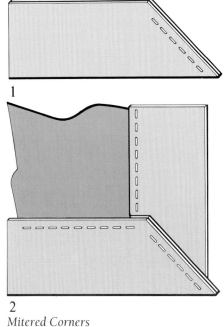

Mitered Corners

Mitered Binding To miter binding at corners, pin and stitch the first strip of binding to the edge of the fabric to be bound, right sides together and stopping ½in (1.25cm) from the corner (**1**). Pull the threads through and knot. Stitch the first strip of binding to the next strip in a right-angled "v" as shown, being careful not to stitch the main piece of fabric as well (**2**). Knot the thread ends. Cut the excess fabric to reduce bulk (**2**). Turn the second binding strip so that it lines up with the next edge of the main fabric and resume stitching, positioning the needle on the seam (**3**). Repeat to attach the other strips of binding. Turn all corners right side out and hem the back of the binding by hand (**4**).

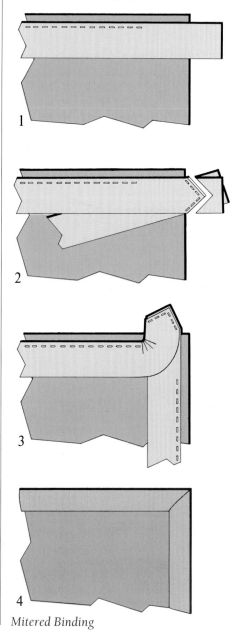

Mitered Binding

Stitching Corners For a neat, pointed corner, first stitch to the exact point at which you want your corner, leaving the needle in the fabric. Raise the presser foot and pivot the fabric 90°; replace the presser foot and continue stitching. When you have finished stitching, trim the seam allowance across the corner to reduce bulk as illustrated below.

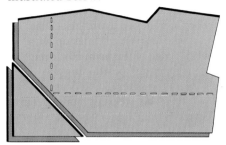

Stitching Corners

Stitching Binding at Corners Sew two strips of binding to opposite edges (**1**). Sew the other two strips onto the other edges so that they go on top of the first strips of binding at the corners. Tuck in the excess fabric at the ends (trim first if there is a lot of excess to reduce bulk) and stitch over the end to strengthen and neaten (**2**).

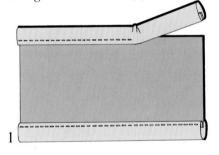

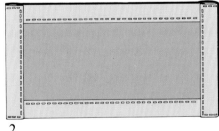

Stitching Binding at Corners

Stitching Curves A curved seam requires careful guidance as it passes under the needle so that the entire seamline ends up the same distance from the raw edge. In order to make the seam lie flat when turned right side out, you should clip into the curves with a pair of scissors after sewing, being

careful not to cut the stitching itself. For curves that will be convex or outward when turned right side out, make small slits into the seam allowance (**A**). For curves that will be concave or inward when right side out, cut out small notches to reduce bulk (**B**).

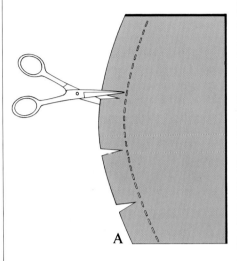

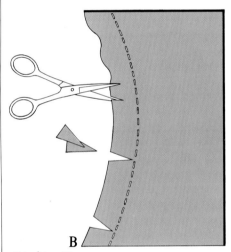

Stitching Curves

Basic Sewing Techniques

Choosing the Needle, Thread, and Stitch Length The type of needle, thread, and stitch length you should use depends upon the fabric you are stitching. For all of the projects in this book, you should use a regular, sharp-point needle. These come in a range of sizes from fine to coarse. As a general rule, use a finer needle for lightweight fabrics, a medium-sized needle for midweight fabrics, and a coarser needle for heavier fabrics. For all projects, normal sewing thread is suitable, but avoid polyester thread on fabrics where you will use a hot iron. The stitch

length you select should vary according to the weight, texture, and structure of the fabric you are stitching. As a general rule, the heavier the fabric, the longer the stitch should be. Refer to the manufacturers' instructions for precise guidelines on using your machine.

Making Bias Binding Bias binding provides a neat and practical finish to many soft furnishings. It can be bought ready-made, but if it is not available in the fabric, color, or width that you require, you can make it yourself following the instructions given below.

Fold your fabric in half diagonally so that the straight edge on the crosswise grain is parallel to the lengthwise grain or selvage (**1**). Press the fabric across the diagonal fold and open out. Using the crease as a guide, mark parallel lines across the fabric, spacing them at the width required for your binding (**2**). Cut along the marked lines to produce bias strips.

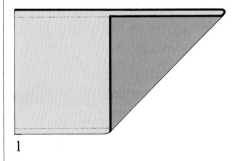

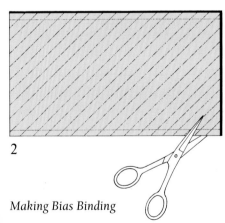

Making Bias Binding

To join bias strips together, trim the edges of each piece along the straight grain and mark ¼in (6mm) seam-lines. Pin the two strips right sides together, matching seamlines. Stitch and press seams open. Trim the protruding corners to align with the edge of the strip. If you are using patterned fabric, make sure the pattern matches up when joining the bias strips.

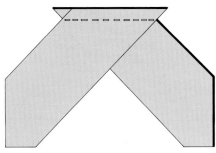

Joining Bias Strips

Making and Attaching Piping To make piping, wrap and pin a strip of bias binding around the piping cord, with wrong sides together, with ⅜in (1cm) seam allowance. Using a zipper foot and positioning the needle to the left of the foot, stitch close to the cord, taking care not to stitch into the piping cord.

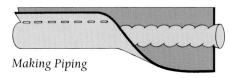

Making Piping

To attach piping, lay the piping on top of the right side of one of the pieces to be seamed so that the piping's seam allowance aligns with the edge of the fabric. Pin the other piece of fabric on top of the piping, right side facing the piping. Using a zipper foot, stitch along the seam just inside the piping stitches. At corners, cut notches out of the seam allowance to reduce bulk and make it lie flat.

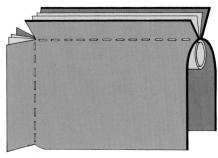

Attaching Piping

Making Pleats There are a number of different types of pleat. In this book (see the Cupboard Curtain and the Kilim Print Door Curtain) we use the knife pleat, where all the pleats lie in the same direction. To make knife pleats, pinch a fold of fabric to twice

the width you want the finished pleat to be, turn it over either to the right or left and pin and stitch it to the curtain. To calculate the amount of fabric the pleats will use up, allow twice the width of the pleat extra for every pleat there is. For example, if you want 10 pleats, each 2in (5cm) wide, you should allow an extra 40in (100cm) of fabric width for the pleats. If, as with the Cupboard Curtain, you want the pleats to go the whole way across the window or door, you need three times the width for the pleated area.

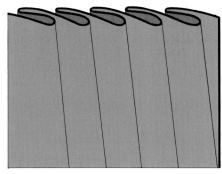

Making Pleats

Fastenings

Buttons When attaching buttons it is important to make sure that they are not attached too tightly. You can prevent this by stitching your button over a matchstick or toothpick. Begin by taking a few stitches at the mark where you want your button. Center the button over the mark, place the stick over the button, and sew the button in position through the holes. After a few stitches from back to front, slide the stick free. Lift the button away from the fabric so that the stitches are pulled taut. Finish by winding the thread firmly around the stitches under the button to create a shank. Knot neatly on the wrong side.

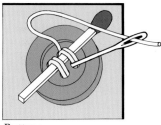

Buttons

Ties Ties make attractive fastenings for duvet covers and pillows. To make them, fold 1¼–2in (3–5cm) wide bias

strips (wider for duvet covers and narrower for pillows) in half lengthwise, wrong sides together, and turn under the raw edges at the sides and at the ends. Stitch together along the long edge and ends and press.

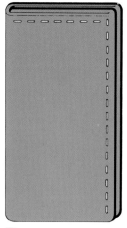

Ties

Zips You can insert zips across the back of a cushion cover or in one of its seams. First measure and mark the exact length of the opening, using your zip as a guide. At both ends, stitch the seam right sides together, with a ½in (1.25cm) seam allowance, up to the opening. Press open a ½in (1.25cm) seam allowance for the zip and pin the zip in place on top of it, making sure the zip pull is facing the outside (downward) and the tape is flat. Turn the cushion over and, using a zipper foot, stitch through all three layers – cushion cover, seam allowance, and zip tape – down both sides of the zip. Finish by pulling the threads through to the wrong side and tying in a reef knot. When stitching the cushion back to the front, leave the zip partially open so that you can turn the cushion cover right side out.

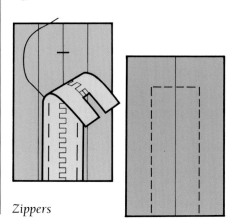

Zippers

Templates

Flying Geese Cushion and Quilt

The two templates on the left are for the Flying Geese Cushion (see p. 94) and the two on the right are for the Flying Geese Quilt (see pp. 36–41). All the templates allow for a ⅜in (1 cm) seam all around and the dotted lines are the stitching lines. To make the templates, transfer the triangles onto cardboard with tracing paper and then cut them out.

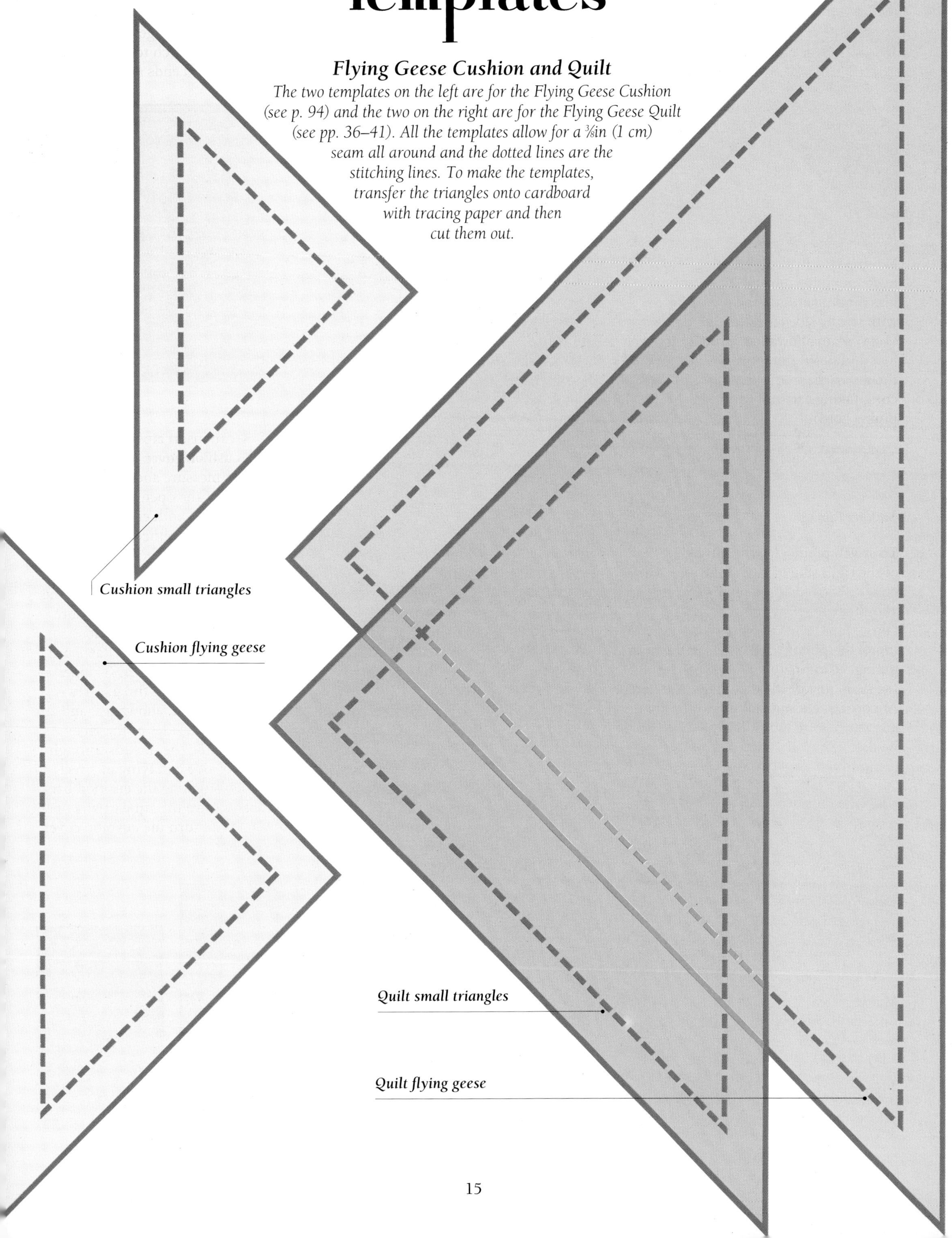

Cushion small triangles

Cushion flying geese

Quilt small triangles

Quilt flying geese

Café Curtain

*The template on the left is for the
decorative scallops (semicircles) at the top
of the Café Curtain (see pp. 60–63). To
make the template, transfer the semicircle
onto cardboard with tracing paper and cut
it out. You can shrink or enlarge the
semicircle to fit the size of your curtain or
the pattern of the fabric by using
a photocopier.*

Tartan Baby Quilt

*The templates below are for the hearts on the squares and at the
corners of the Tartan Baby Quilt (see pp. 46–51). To make the
templates, transfer the hearts onto cardboard with tracing paper
and cut them out. The smaller template for the corner hearts
allows for a ¼in (6mm) seam all around and the dotted line is the
stitching line. You can use the alphabet opposite if you want to
appliqué your child's initials onto the quilt instead of the hearts.
You can shrink or enlarge the letters to fit the size of the squares
on the quilt by using a photocopier.*

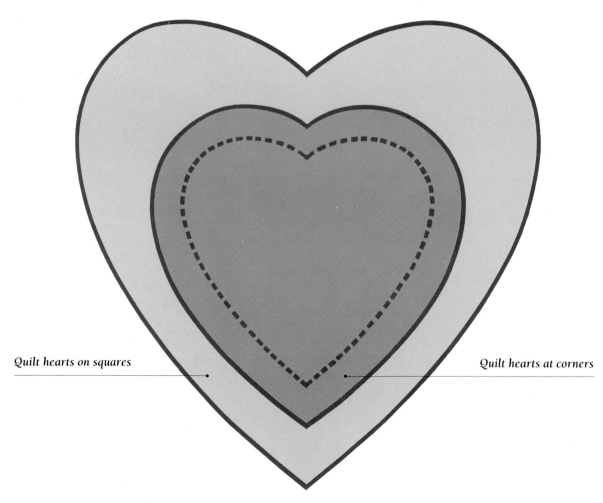

Quilt hearts on squares

Quilt hearts at corners

Embroidered Good Morning Cushion

The alphabet template (below) and the bluebird and morning glory design (below and opposite) are for the Embroidered Good Morning Cushion (see p. 94). Use dressmaker's carbon paper to transfer the design and whatever message you want directly onto the front cover of the cushion. Complete the stitching in stem stitch (see p. 11), using an embroider's frame to keep your work flat.

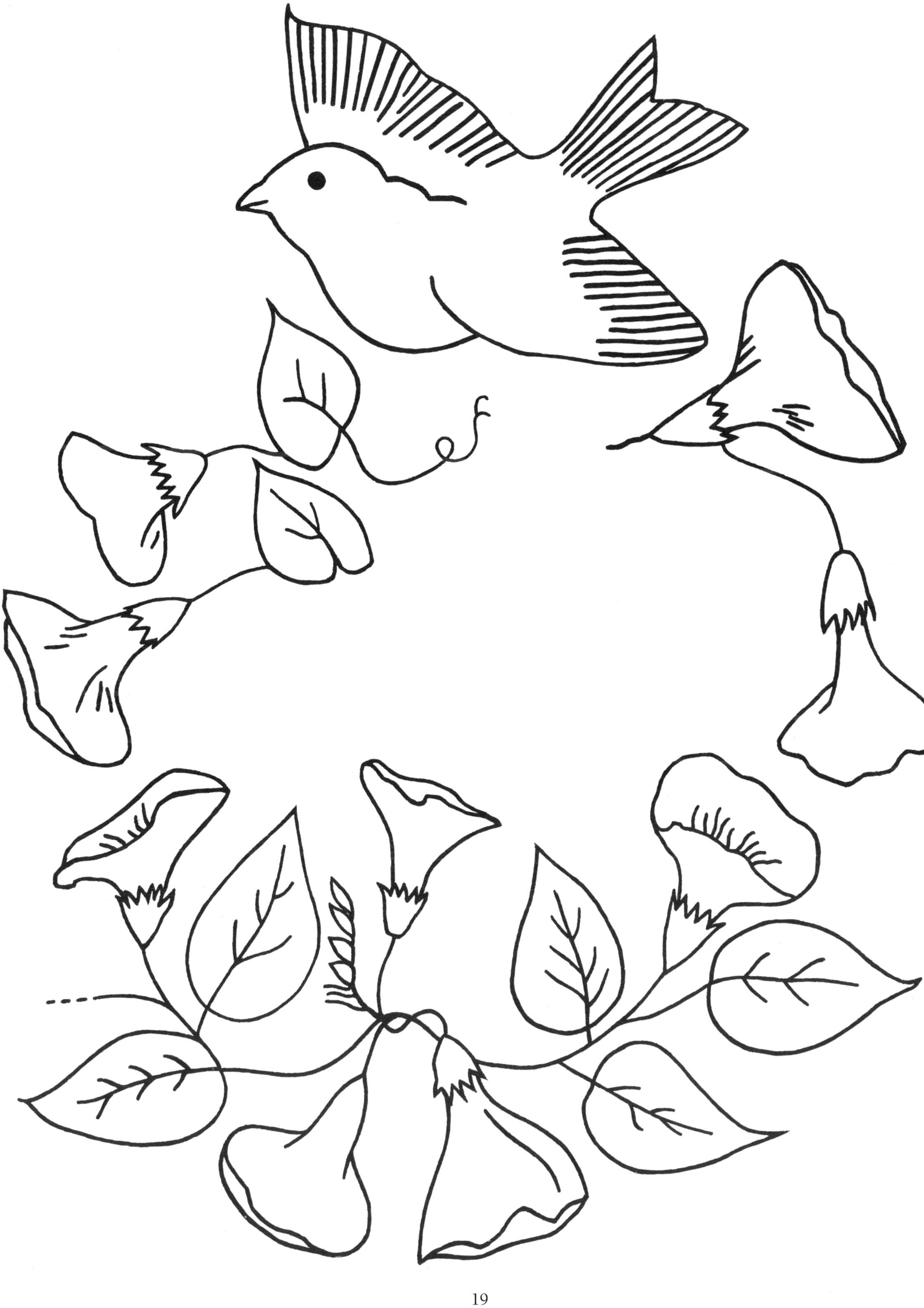

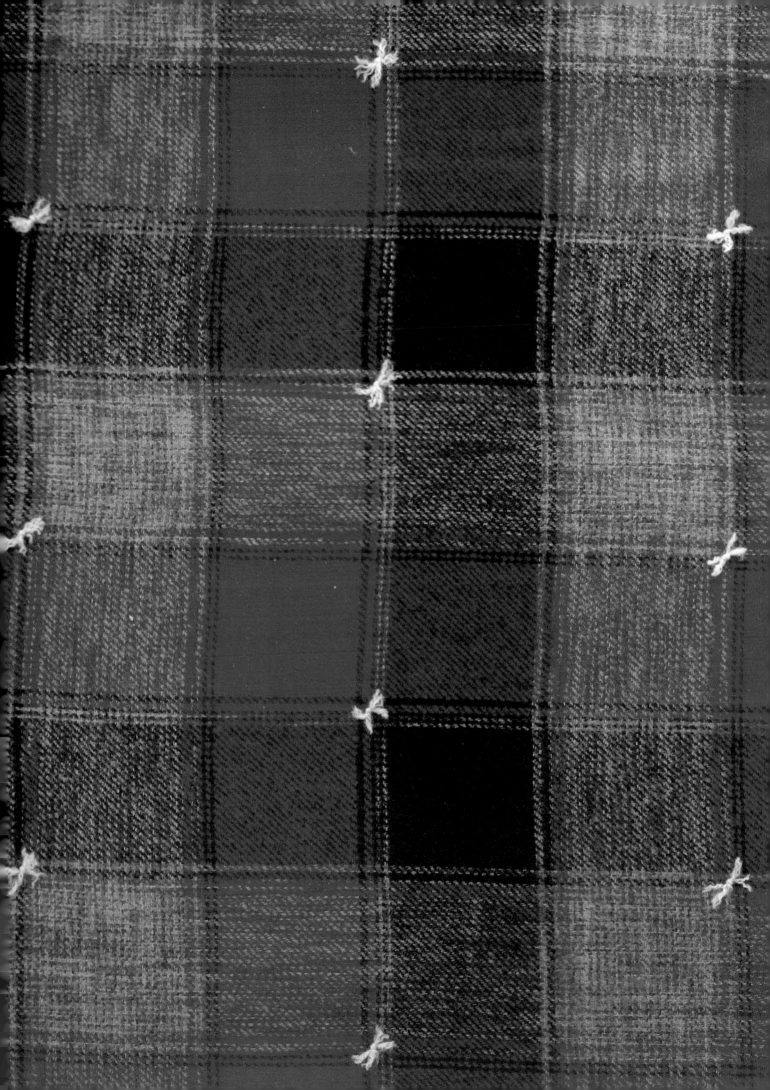

BEDDING

Striped Duvet Cover

*An understated classic – a simple duvet cover in the style of
a traditional coverlet from northern England, without the
elaborate quilting.*

DURING THE NINETEENTH CENTURY, the north-east of England was the home of a wonderfully simple, striking, and strangely unique style of pieced quilt – known as the Durham Strippy. In their original form, these quilts were examples of boldness, elegance, and finesse akin to Shaker quilts – Turkey red and white stripes were a favorite combination, five red and four white, roughly nine inches (23 centimetres) wide. The backing was usually a single width of fabric, and the top and underside were quilted together with time-consuming complexities of feathers, diamonds, leaves, lovers' knots, and flowers to hold the filling – which was usually lambs' or sheep's wool – securely in place.

The traditional fabrics used were dress cottons in solid colors or small floral, sprigged or parsley patterns. Linen and wool were also used occasionally. The earliest example is of scarlet and black wool, and was made in the Isle of Man in the mid-nineteenth century.

In deference to our more hurried times, we have dispensed with fine quilting, and used fresh, cool colors to translate the strippy into a modern duvet cover. The wide stripes in the duvet top mirror the design of the brass bed, and the sharp black binding reinforces the visual link between the two. There are also decorative ties, which are made of the same fabric as the underside for the bottom ties and as the duvet top's darker stripes for the top ties. But the essential components of the strippy are retained, along with its classic appeal.

Whatever combination you choose, remember that the result is most effective when there is a clear contrast, whether of color or pattern, between the stripes.

MATERIALS
For a duvet cover measuring 88in (224cm) square

Cotton for duvet top lighter stripes: 2½yd (2.25m) of 45in (115cm) fabric

Cotton for duvet top darker stripes, ties, and facing: 5yd (4.6m) of 45in (115cm) fabric

Cotton for duvet underside (joined down middle), ties, and facing: 5yd (4.6m) of 45in (115cm) fabric

Black cotton for piping: 1¼yd (1.15m) of 45in (115cm) fabric

Piping cord: 9⅓yd (8.5m)

Sewing thread matching the colors of the stripes and underside

Duvet top lighter stripe

The Fabrics
A cool, calm harmony of bamboo, ivory, and parchment colors, with a sharp black binding for contrast.

Duvet underside

Duvet binding

Duvet top darker stripe

Making the Duvet Cover

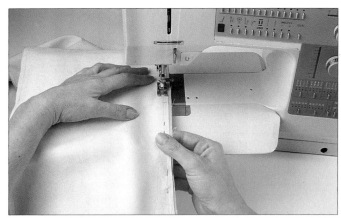

1 Cut 4 strips of the lighter fabric, each 10½in (27cm) wide, 88¾in (226cm) long, and 5 strips of the darker fabric the same size for the cover top. Pin and stitch right sides of strips together leaving a ⅜in (1cm) seam allowance, alternating light and dark so that a dark strip is on each outside edge.

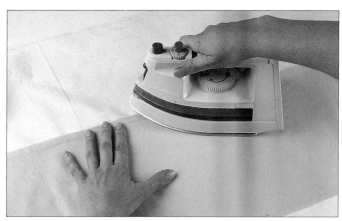

2 Once you have stitched all 9 strips together, press the 8 seams flat in the direction of the lighter strips.

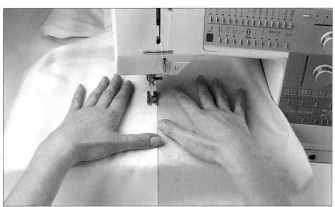

3 Overstitch on the right side with thread matching the lighter cotton to strengthen the seam and prevent fraying.

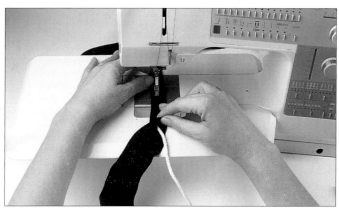

4 For the piping, cut strips of bias binding 2in (5cm) wide and join them to make one continuous strip at least 30ft (9m) long. Using the zipper foot, stitch around piping cord (see p. 14 for piping and binding techniques).

5 To make the ties, cut 6 strips of the darker top fabric, each 2in (5cm) wide, 18½in (47cm) long. Fold them in half lengthwise, turning under the raw edges by ¼in (6mm) down the sides and at the ends and stitch to make ¾in (2cm) wide ties. Pin the piping to the bottom end of the cover top and pin the 6 tie strips over the piping at about 10½in (27cm) intervals.

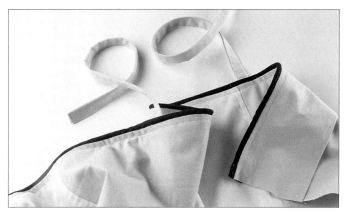

6 For the top facing, cut a strip of the darker top fabric, 4in (10cm) wide, 88¾in (226cm) long. Pin, tack, and, with the zipper foot, stitch facing to top, right sides together, over the piping and ties. Turn, press, and topstitch as shown. Cut the underside fabric to the same size as the duvet top. Repeat steps 5 and 6 to attach ties and facing to the underside (omitting the piping). Make sure the ties' positions match those on the cover top.

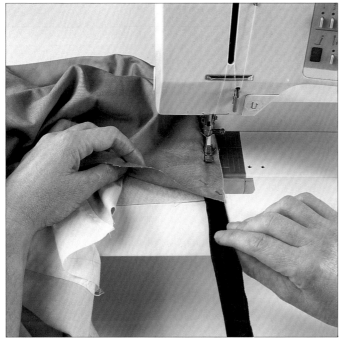

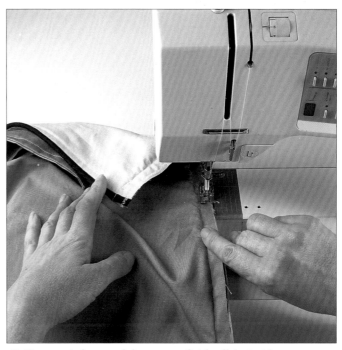

7 *Pin cover top to underside right sides together, with piping in between as shown. Stitch around the remaining 3 sides of the cover with zipper foot, taking special care at the corners, and overstitching the facings at the opening.*

8 *Zigzag stitch around the seam to finish off the inside raw edges. Turn right side out and press. Hand-hem the facings.*

Variation

Savannah Print

Using harmonizing prints for the strips on the duvet top creates a more contemporary look. This combination of chevrons and an animal print, with crisp, natural cotton for the underside, evokes the spirit of Africa and would look good bound in black. Small spots, stripes, florals, or even bold, plain fabric would all offer a nice contrast too.

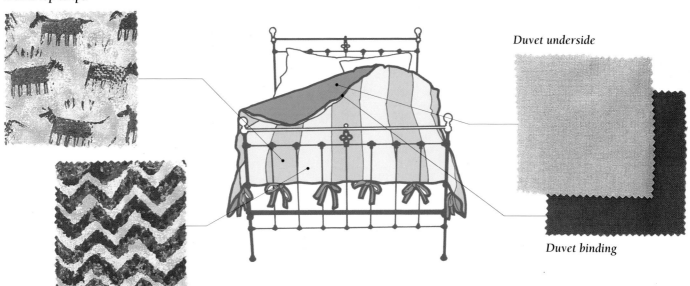

Duvet top stripe

Duvet top stripe

Duvet underside

Duvet binding

Alsace Checked Bed Linen

*The crisp, clean partnership of red and blue checks, set off by a
navy undersheet and natural calico, makes inviting bedding
that might have come straight from the wooded valleys of
northeast France.*

ALSACE IS A HIDDEN CORNER in northeast France, full of charm and character, held in a time warp that transports the visitor to medieval times without the discomfort. Outside, the ancient streets are cobbled, and within the typical Alsatian home there is a sense of warmth and welcome. Neat and orderly, the house is likely to radiate the old-fashioned virtues of good housekeeping – an abundance of white linen and lace sets off the dark polished wood furniture. But most appealing of all are the bedrooms, with carved wooden beds – and even occasional boxbeds – topped with puffy duvets, resplendent in a livery of indigo or scarlet checks.

These pillowcases and duvet cover are made from Kelsch, an indigenous fabric originally woven from coarse cotton and linen. Simplicity is the first impression – and this bedding is very simple to make – but there is also a sense of rightness that comes from a classic. Small touches, such as the contrasting lining and button bands allow for an interplay of different colors and checks, and give a sense of crisp definition which never goes out of fashion.

Alsace bed linen as it appears here – with a dark blue undersheet and matching dark blue and white checked cloths covering the bedside table – is right for a boy. Given a white undersheet and a lace tablecloth, it can also look very feminine. It works in modern urban setting, as well as with modern country pine. It is a style to which it is easy to become addicted, and checks, big or small, scarlet or blue, have the virture of marrying well.

MATERIALS

*For two pillowcases measuring
17¾in (45cm) × 27½in (70cm)*

Cotton for pillowcases: 2¾yd
(2.5m) of 45in (115cm) fabric
Cotton for buttonbands: 1yd
(0.8m) of 45in (115cm) fabric
Matching sewing thread
¾in (2cm) buttons: 6
White button thread

*For a duvet cover measuring
68in (173cm) × 91½in (232cm)*
Cotton for duvet top (joined
down middle): 4yd (3.5m) of
45in (115cm) fabric
Cotton for duvet underside
(joined down middle): 4yd
(3.5m) of 45in (115cm) fabric
Cotton for buttonband (joined
down middle): 1yd (0.8m) of
45in (115cm) fabric
Matching sewing thread
¾in (2cm) buttons: 5
Red button thread

The Fabrics

*A fresh, classic collection of colors in a familiar but
unbeatable partnership. Red, white, and blue always
combine well, and bring a bracing gust of seaside air
as a positive start to the day.*

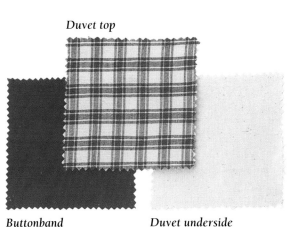

Duvet top

Buttonband

Duvet underside

Pillowcase

Buttonband

Making the Pillows and Duvet Cover

The process for making the pillows is shown below. The duvet cover is made in exactly the same way except it requires three seams instead of two since the duvet top and underside consist of two different pieces of fabric. The trim size for the duvet top and underside is 68¾in (175cm) × 88¾in (225cm). The trim size for the two pieces for the buttonband is 7¾in (20cm) × 68¾in (175cm).

1 *Cut a piece of fabric 18½in (47cm) × 48¾in (124cm) for the pillow and 2 strips 7¾in (20cm) × 18½in (47cm) for the buttonband. Stitch a buttonband strip to each of the 2 short sides of pillowcase fabric, right sides together with a ⅜in (1cm) seam allowance. Press the seams towards the band.*

2 *Fold the pillowcase in half, right sides together. Pin and stitch down each long side of the pillowcase with a ⅜in (1cm) seam allowance. Make sure that the checks in front and back match up and that the band seams are pressed towards the band.*

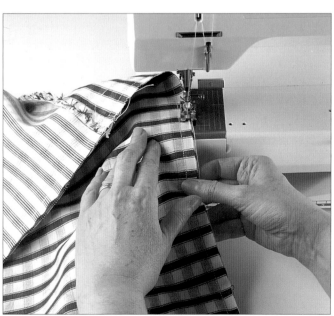

3 *Zigzag stitch down the raw edges of the 2 long seams to strengthen and neaten. Fold band over to wrong side and pin in place with a ⅜in (1cm) seam allowance, ensuring that band on wrong side is ¼in (6mm) lower than on right side.*

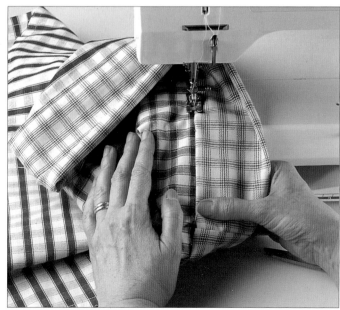

4 *Press band and stitch in a "ditch" from the right side, catching the band beneath. Draw any thread ends through to inside, knot and darn in place. Press. Make buttonholes (see opposite above) and sew buttons in place.*

Making Buttonholes

Buttonholes make a tidy closure for pillowcases and duvet covers. If buttonholes are set into an applied band as here, the double thickness of the fabric helps prevent the gaps between the buttons from gaping. The buttonholes for the duvet cover (below) are made in exactly the same way as for the pillows except the duvet cover needs five buttons instead of three because it has a wider opening. See page 14 for techniques on sewing on buttons.

1 *Place 3 equidistant buttons along pillowcase band at 4½in (11.5cm) intervals. Pin to mark size and position of buttonholes.*

2 *Using small stitches, tack around where the buttonhole will be cut to hold the 2 layers of fabric in place and mark the length.*

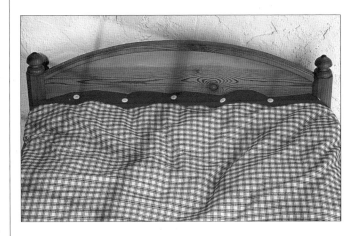

3 *With a stitch ripper or sharp embroidery scissors, cut neatly within the tacking stitches.*

4 *Sewing over taut waxed double thread, buttonhole stitch (see p. 11) around sides and overstitch at ends. Pull waxed thread taut and cut away surplus.*

Variation

Terracotta and Cream

Two small Provençal prints make lively alternatives for the main fabric of the duvet and pillowcase. The matching stripe used as a buttonband provides a link between the two and gives crisp definition to both.

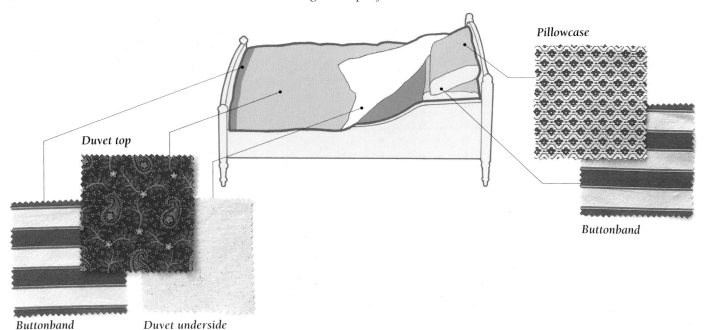

Pillowcase

Duvet top

Buttonband

Buttonband   *Duvet underside*

Buttonband

Dutch Paisley Duvet Cover

A lavish duvet cover inspired by Dutch quilts of exotically patterned Indian fabrics imported by traders in the seventeenth century.

BESIDES HAVING AN indigenous tradition for fine woolen and linen textiles, the Dutch imported exotic fabrics from further afield via the Dutch East India Company from its foundation in 1602. The fine wood-block printed cottons and silks of India were particularly prized, and well-to-do merchants from Amsterdam and Rotterdam slept sweetly in their carved wooden beds beneath palampores fashioned from pieced and mitered strips of intricate paisleys and tree of life designs in a rich harmony of color. Until a bit of successful industrial espionage by the French in the nineteenth century and the discovery of colorfast chemical dyes, India was the main source of subtle rainbow-hued textiles which did not fade with the sun or wash out with water – Indian dyers had the secret of mordants, that fix the color in the fabric.

This duvet cover, with a central panel edged with two bands of contrasting prints, shows how you can combine unrelated patterns successfully provided color and design scale are carefully considered.

The duvet cover's richness of color and pattern harmonizes beautifully with the ethnic feel of the room's rug and table cover, as well as the warm mahogany bed. But you could take the principle of mixing and matching prints to create quite a different mood. The soft, antique colors of Jacobean inspired fabrics would give a medieval feel, while a combination of patterns in fresh blue and white would produce a more modern, seaside look. Light, bright shades can be just as striking as deep, rich ones, but remember that you need fairly definite contrasts of tone and pattern so that the final effect looks designed rather than haphazard.

MATERIALS
For a duvet cover measuring 88in (224cm) square

Patterned cotton for outer border and facing: 2½yd (2.25m) of 45in (115cm) fabric
Patterned cotton for inner border: 2¼yd (2m) of 45in (115cm) fabric
Patterned cotton for center square: 1⅔yd (1.5m) of 60in (150cm) fabric
Cotton for underside (joined down middle) and facing: 5¼yd (4.6m) of 45in (115cm) fabric
Ready-made gold piping braid: 10yd (9m)
Toggle buttons: 6
Gold braid for button loops: ¼yd (25cm)
Black sewing thread

For tassels
Embroidery thread for tassels: 6 hanks in 3 colors
Gold thread for binding tassels: 3yd (2.75m)

The Fabrics

A paisley design of muted red, brown, and blue is contained inside two different boldly patterned borders, which are harmonized by their black and white color scheme. The red is echoed in the striped underside, adding to the feeling of opulence with its warm tones of yellow ocher.

Duvet top outer border

Duvet top center square

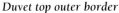

Duvet underside

Duvet top inner border

COMPONENTS

Below are the elements needed for an 88in (224cm) square duvet cover

Duvet top outer border:
4 strips, each 7¾in
(19.5cm) wide, 88¾in
(226cm) long, with
ends cut across
diagonally at 45°

Duvet top inner border:
4 strips, each 10¾in
(27.5cm) wide, 74¾in
(191cm) long, with
ends cut across
diagonally at 45°

Tassels: 6 hanks six-
strand embroidery
thread and gold thread

Duvet top center
square: 54¾in
(140cm) square

Facing for duvet
tops and underside:
each 3in (7.5cm)
wide, 88¾in
(226cm) long

Duvet underside:
88¾in (226cm)
square

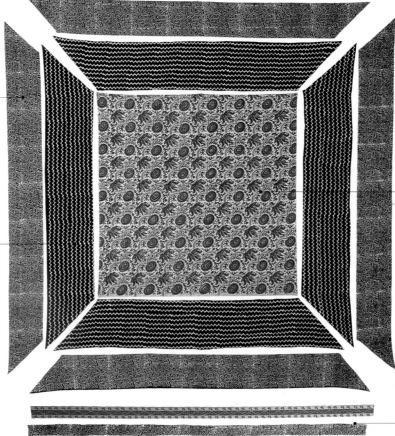

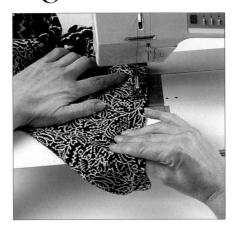

Making the Duvet Cover

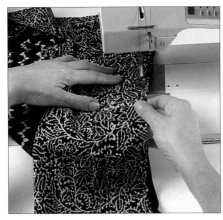

1 Cut all the fabric following the
components photograph. Pin and sew
each outer border of duvet top to its inner
border, right sides together, with ⅜in
(1cm) seams so that when the seams are
pressed open, the edges and the diagonals
at the corners match.

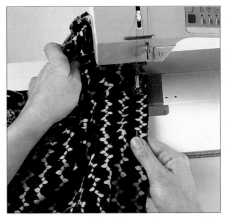

2 Stitch together the bias-cut corners,
matching the seams and taking care
not to stretch the fabric too much (see
p. 12 for mitering techniques). Leave each
inside corner seam open ⅝in (1.5cm) for
attaching center square and overstitch
for strength.

3 Zigzag raw edges of center square and
pin it in position following the
components photograph. Stitch the center
square in place right sides together,
tacking it first to make sure of fit. Press all
seams open.

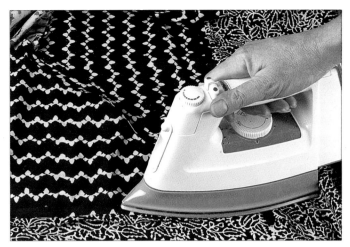

4 *Sew facing strip along opening end of duvet underside, right sides together. Turn, press and hem.*

5 *Along the opening end of the duvet top, tack the piping (see p. 14 for piping techniques), decorative edge facing right side in. Pin loops of gold braid a bit smaller than the length of the toggle to the piping on the duvet top, the loops pointing inwards and their ends sticking out. Here we used 6 loops at 14in (35.5cm) intervals. Overstitch the cut ends of the piping to prevent it from fraying.*

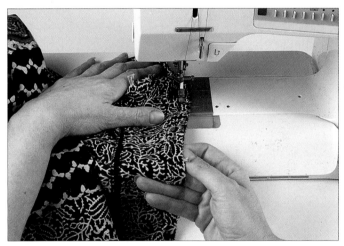

6 *Pin facing for duvet top in place, right sides together, with piping in between and all seam edges aligning. Tack in place and stitch, using a zipper foot. Turn right side out, press, and hem.*

7 *Making sure that the faced opening edges are together, pin the other three sides of the top to the underside, right sides facing, pinning the piping in place as you go and being generous with it at the corners. Overstitch the opening for strength.*

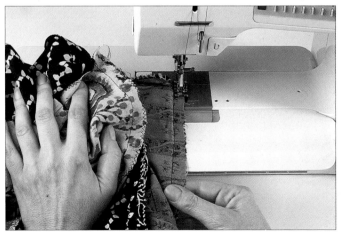

8 *Turn right side out to check work, then turn inside out again and zigzag stitch all the raw edges together.*

9 *Mark with a pin or marking pen the positions of the toggles on the duvet underside, making sure they match the positions of the loops.*

Making the Duvet Cover (cont.)

10 *Stitch the toggles securely in place using heavy-duty thread or double thickness sewing cotton.*

11 *Stitch on the tassels at the corners (see below for instructions on making tassels).*

Making Tassels

Tassels are one of the simplest ways to add glamour to your sewing. To make the 12 tassels for this duvet, you need 6 hanks of six-strand embroidery thread (a hank makes 2 tassels) and 3 yards (2.75 meters) of gold embroidery thread. Try to get embroidery thread in colors that match those found in the duvet itself.

1 *To make 2 tassels, first knot 2 2in (5cm) lengths of thread to make 2 small loops, leaving enough room on ends for tying.*

2 *Knot the loop ends securely to both ends of a hank of embroidery thread.*

3 *Wind gold embroidery thread tightly around each end of the hank, just below the loop.*

4 *Finish off by stitching the gold thread into the top of the loop securely.*

5 *Cut the hank in half to form 2 tassels and trim the cut ends evenly. Repeat the process until you have the required amount of tassels.*

Variations

Study in Blue

For a breezy seaside look, use this combination of fresh blue and white patterns made shipshape by a neat stripe. Here, the center square is in a small print, the outer border in glorious swirling flowers, and the underside in a darker solid blue.

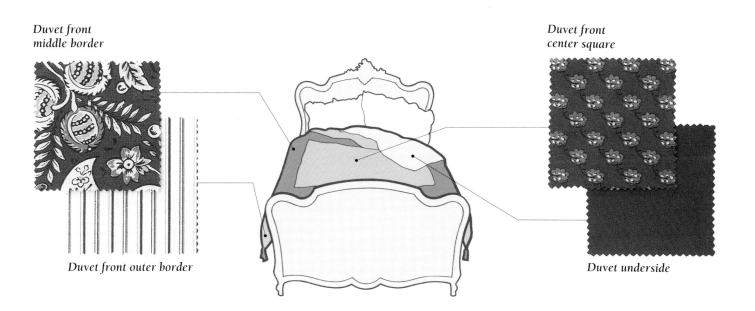

Duvet front
middle border

Duvet front
center square

Duvet front outer border

Duvet underside

Four Poster Bedding

Richly patterned, Jacobean-inspired fabrics suit dark, wood surroundings, and these soft antique colors would be ideal dressing for a four-poster bed. The patterned stripe separates the prancing horses decorating the center panel from the magnificent feathers of the outer border. The underside continues the theme with a warm sandy yellow print of small medieval creatures.

Duvet front
middle border

Duvet front
center square

Duvet front outer border

Duvet underside

Flying Geese Quilt

A traditional American design, this quilt is clean, crisp, and easy to make, and the perfect way to recycle scraps rescued from worn clothing.

THE FLYING GEESE MOTIF found its way to America from Great Britain, where it was used along with other border patterns for pieced medallion quilts. After its transatlantic crossing, it continued to be used in this way, but the charm of the vigorous triangles chasing each other gradually became the attraction in its own right, and young girls would begin stitching for their hope chest with a quilt of stripes and triangles, pieced from the tiny printed fabrics that made up the voluminous gowns of the time. It continues to be the perfect way to use all those shirts whose sleeves have begun to wear thin, or the snippets of fabric remaining from home sewing stints.

The larger triangles can be as varied as you like, as long as there is a unifying common denominator of color, and the patterns – whether stripes, checks, flowers, or paisleys – are of similar density. The completed design works best if you confine the small triangles to one paler color, and make the stripes from a darker contrast. (If you use solids instead of patterns, however, you can break these rules as in the variation on page 41.)

With care it is possible to cut multiple triangles from folded fabric all at once (see page 10), but it is important to ensure that they are all identical in size and match your template. Also, it is vital to keep to the same seam allowance when sewing, because a small error repeated over many triangles will compound into a discrepancy between the length of the plain strips and the flying geese. However, you may be able to rectify this by adding or subtracting a goose.

MATERIALS

For a quilt measuring 76½in (193cm) × 88in (224cm)

Striped cotton for front stripes: 2½yd (2.3m) of 36in (90cm) fabric

Lawn for small triangles: 2¾yd (2.6m) of 36in (90cm) fabric

Lawn for flying geese: 2¾yd (2.6cm) of 36in (90cm) fabric

Striped cotton for underside: 5yd (4.6m) of 45in (115cm) fabric

Plain cotton for binding: 1⅔yd (1.5m) of 45in (115cm) fabric

Wadding for interlining: 5yd (4.6m) of 45in (115cm) fabric

Red and white sewing thread

The Fabrics

Fine, crisp Egyptian cotton, in myriad stripes of red, white, and blue, spiked with a scarlet binding.

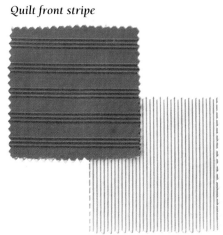

Quilt front stripe

Quilt front small triangles

Quilt underside

Quilt binding

Quilt front flying geese

COMPONENTS

Below are the elements needed for an 88in (224cm) × 76½in (193cm) quilt

Quilt front large flying geese:
90 triangles 11¼in × 8in ×
8in (28.5cm × 20cm × 20cm)
– see template on p. 15

Quilt front small triangles:
180 triangles 8in × 5⅝in ×
5⅝in (20cm × 14cm × 14cm)
– see template on p. 15

Quilt front stripe:
4 strips 6¾in
(17cm) wide, 88¾in
(226cm) long

Quilt underside:
2 strips 39in
(98.5cm) wide ×
88¾in (226cm)
long, to be joined
together.

Binding: 4 2in (5cm) wide strips,
2 strips 89in (226.6cm) long, and
2 strips 77½in (195cm) long

Making the Quilt

1 Using the 2 templates on p. 15, trace and cut 90 large triangles and 180 smaller triangles (see p. 10 for multiple cutting techniques). The templates allow for ⅜in (1cm) seam around each triangle.

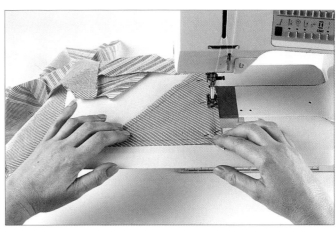

2 Pin and sew the long edge of a small triangle to the shorter edge of a large triangle, right sides together, so that the stripes make a right angle when opened out. Match corners exactly and stitch without stretching the material.

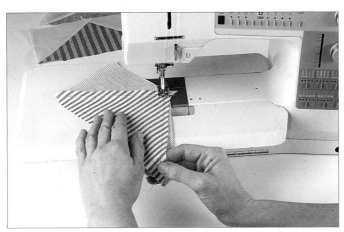

3 Attach the longer edge of another small triangle to the other short edge of the large triangle, right sides together. The point of the large triangle should come ⅜in (1cm) below the top of the resulting rectangle.

4 Repeat the process until all triangles have been combined into rectangles and then press them as shown here.

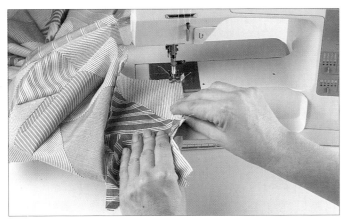

5 Arrange all the rectangles on the floor in the pattern you want (we have gone for a "random" effect). Stitch them right sides together in this arrangement until you have 5 strips of 18 rectangles each. Make sure that the point of the large triangle is exactly on the seam line. Press with points up.

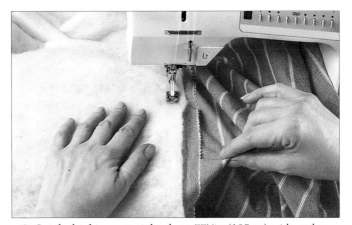

6 Cut the backing material at least 77¼in (195cm) wide and to the same length as the pieced strips (about 88⅜in [226cm]). If backing fabric is not wide enough to use in one piece, sew selvage together along center back. Press seam open (or if fabric is in one piece fold in half lengthwise and press fold). Place wadding up against center seam (or fold) and pin and stitch.

Making the Quilt (cont.)

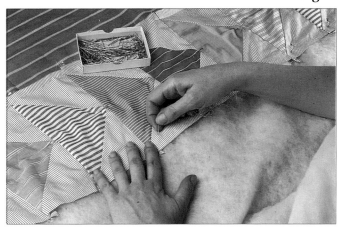

7 Pin a strip of triangles so that triangle points line up over center seam of underside, wrong sides together. Smoothing in place with your hand, pin the outer corners of the triangles in place making sure to go through top, wadding, and underside.

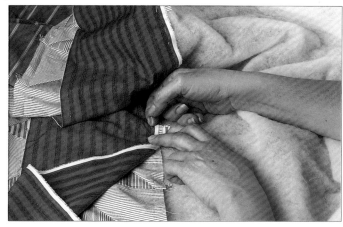

8 Cut the unpieced strips and pin 1 on top of the triangle strip so that right sides are together. To insure accuracy, tack all 4 layers together, checking there are no tucks or wrinkles. Stitch exactly along the outer triangle points.

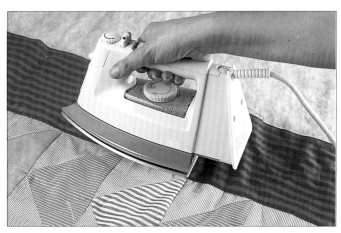

9 Remove tacking, turn unpieced strip right side up and press flat, pinning in position as you go. Check both top and underside when you press to ensure that you have not caught any fabric unintentionally.

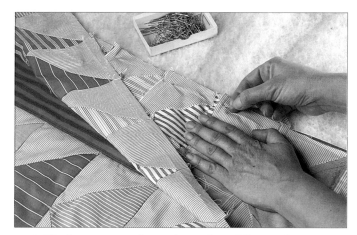

10 Pin the next strip of triangles in place, following the procedure in steps 8 and 9. Take care that the triangles point in the same direction as the first strip and that the triangles in each strip line up with each other.

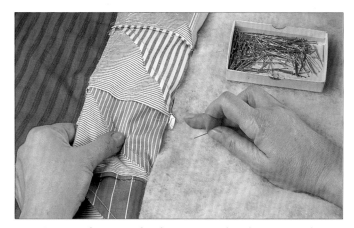

11 Once you have completed sewing together the strips on the first half (3 pieced strips and 2 unpieced strips), place another length of wadding up against the center back seam, pinning it in place, and repeat steps 7 through 12 to complete the second half.

12 Cut and join the binding fabric into 2 strips 2in (5cm) wide, 89in (226.6cm) long (see p. 13 for binding techniques). Press in half lengthwise and pin and sew to sides of quilt, catching top, wadding, and underside. Trim excess fabric and wadding, turn binding over and hem by hand or machine on other side. Press smooth. Make 2 strips for ends, each 77½in (195cm) long, and repeat the process. At the corners turn under the excess and stitch by hand (see p. 13 for techniques on stitching corners).

Variations

Tiny Prints

Crisp, finely patterned lawn cotton is the perfect fabric for patchwork. Here we have chosen a group of diminutive flower prints in shades of toffee, tan, and tobacco brown, with the broad stripes and small triangles in delicate black and white prints. A rich paisley works well for the underside, and the black binding adds a neat finishing touch.

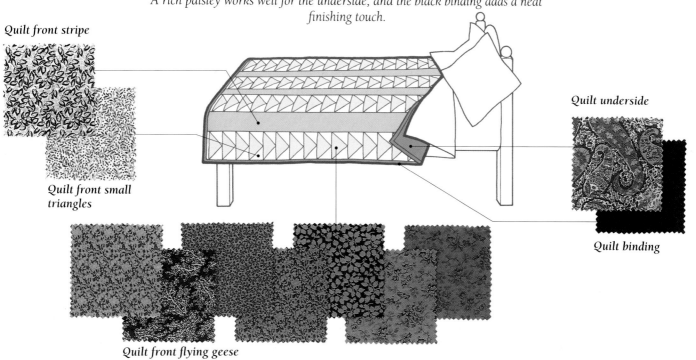

Quilt front stripe

Quilt front small triangles

Quilt underside

Quilt binding

Quilt front flying geese

Amish Plains

A predominance of black was typical of the Amish. Against this background, the bright cottons sing out with full intensity. We have chosen five cottons for the large triangles so that you could use a different color for each strip. A red and white polka dot cotton on the underside picks up the bright red geese on the front.

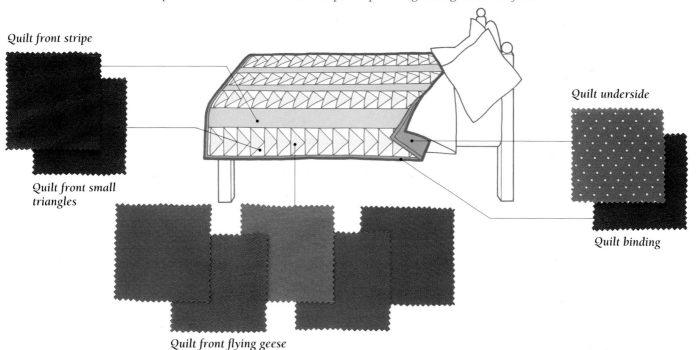

Quilt front stripe

Quilt front small triangles

Quilt underside

Quilt binding

Quilt front flying geese

Shaker Woolen Coverlet

*Fleecy wool in a cheering scarlet and black check, edged with
a broad band of black, makes a cozy coverlet in the handsome,
no-nonsense spirit of the Shakers.*

SHAKER PRODUCTS EMBODIED William Morris's recommendation that one surround oneself only with things that one believes beautiful or knows to be useful. Even the humblest Shaker objects were timeless and uplifting classics, possessing perfect proportions, grace of line, and respectful exploitation of the natural materials.

Like everything else they made, Shaker textiles were plain but good. At the beginning of the nineteenth century they manufactured almost all their own cloth, and they developed an attractive repertoire of stripes, checks and twills woven from cotton, silk, linen, and various experimental fibers such as raccoon and cat fur spun and knitted with silk for strength. Dyeing was a summer operation undertaken in vast quantities – it was not unusual to tackle 176 pounds (80 kilograms) of wool at a time. The resources used by the Shakers had not changed much from those used by Native Americans for centuries – such things as butternut bark, aleppo galls, brazilwood, indigo, fermented sorrel, and sumac berries were transformed into colorfast dyes of surprising brilliance.

Our coverlet, with its quick and easy tufting to hold the three layers of wool together, is inspired by a hand-woven woolen bed cover made in Canterbury in 1880. The Shaker original sported an area of gray-green, surrounded by large checks in scarlet, gray, and dark green, and the top was tufted to a lining of red flannel. Since hand-weaving is beyond the skills of most of us, we have used a warm brushed woolen check to make a coverlet that will withstand the most Arctic cold.

MATERIALS

For a coverlet measuring
78in (198cm) × 88in (224cm)
If you are unable to find 80in
(200cm) wide fabric, buy double
the length of the coverlet and
stitch 2 pieces together

Checked wool for front: 2½yd
(2.3m) of 80in (200cm) fabric
Red wool for backing: 2½yd
(2.3m) of 80in (200cm) fabric
Wool domette for lining: 2½yd
(2.3m) of 80in (200cm) fabric
Black wool for binding: 2yd
(1.85m) of 45in (115cm) fabric
Cream double knitting wool for
tufting: 10yd (9m)
Black sewing thread

The Fabrics
*An extroverted scarlet and black check with a discreet
thread of cream echoed by the tufting. It has been
edged with black and has a soft scarlet backing.*

Coverlet front

Coverlet backing

Coverlet binding

Making the Coverlet

1 Cut out the fabric for the front, interlining, and backing, all at least 74in (188cm) × 84in (214cm). Lay out interlining over backing fabric, stretching it to fit. Next lay checked wool on top and pin all 3 layers together.

2 After making sure that the surface is flat and even, pin and tack around the edges.

3 For the binding, cut binding fabric into strips 5½in (14cm) wide (see p. 13 for binding techniques) and join strips together to make 4 strips, 2 at least 74in (188cm) long for the ends and 2 at least 88½in (225cm) long for the sides.

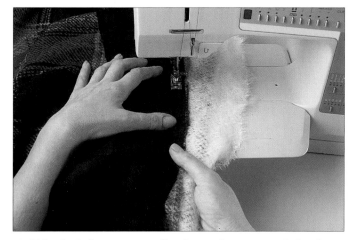

4 Using a damp cloth to protect the wool, press the joining seams of the strips open. Then press the binding in half lengthwise.

5 Take the 2 shorter strips of binding and sew one to the head and one to the foot of the coverlet, right sides facing with a ⅜in (1cm) seam allowance.

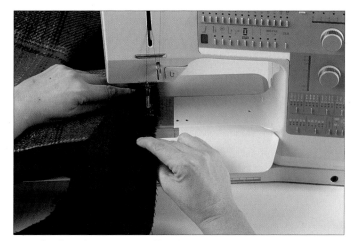

6 Trim any excess fabric, turn binding right side over, and hem by machine on backing side. Press.

7 Take the 2 longer strips of binding and attach them to the edges in the same way, turning under a small hem at each end (see p. 13 for techniques on stitching corners).

8 Overstitch the corners by machine, both to neaten and strengthen the coverlet (see p. 13 for techniques on stitching corners).

9 Mark positions for hand-tied tufting with pins. We have used the check to make a diamond pattern, spacing the tufts at about 10in (25cm) intervals. Stitch through the whole coverlet with a double length of double knitting wool. Knot the ends securely with a reef knot (see p. 11) and cut the wool to 1in (2.5cm), teasing it out to fluff up the fibers.

Variation

Indian Ikat

The Shaker coverlet adapts well to a wide range of fabrics and looks. Here, thick Ikat cotton's flame pattern is echoed in hot colors – red on the front and toffee brown on the back, bound in scarlet, making an attractive summer quilt.

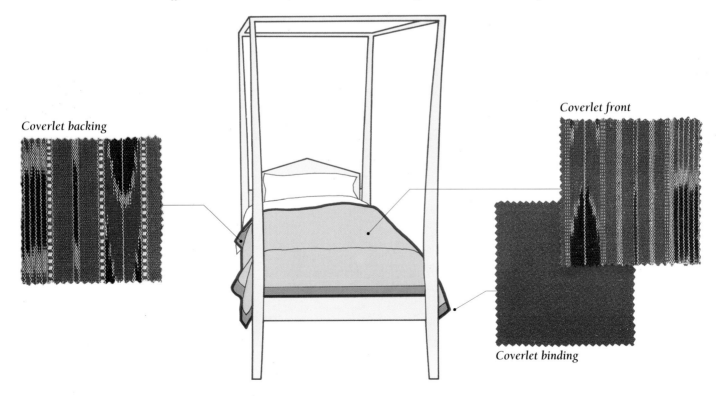

Coverlet backing

Coverlet front

Coverlet binding

Tartan Baby Quilt

Infant chic in strong colors bestrewn with scarlet hearts – this is for a modern baby who cannot resist a nod to nostalgia.

THIS BABY'S QUILT is quick and fun to make, and will probably have won its owner's heart to a devotion that will long outlast the original cot. Our quilt has all the good qualities one could desire – it looks good as a miniature version of the handsome, classic bedclothing beloved of American designers; the cotton and terylene components are easily washed and dry quickly, so that orange juice and milk and other unmentionable stains need not provoke hysteria; it is light and packable and a comforting little bit of home to take away on visits to granny; it happily does its duty as a floor mat to sit on when sussing those fluffy cubes, a comforter in the car, and – in exceptional circumstances – a changing mat with dinky little hearts at each corner to take your mind off the indignities below: altogether a good companion for a smart baby.

If hearts are not your cup of tea then you could appliqué scotty dogs, bows, or sun-bonnet Sue's to the front, or embroider the baby's name on the quilt, using the template on page 16. You can also vary the colors to suit the room for which the quilt is intended.

Bear in mind that whatever work of art you create, it will get plenty of hard wear. It is likely to be chewed, dragged along the ground, and even folded lovingly and grubbily around favorite teddy bears and the dog, so finish it carefully, avoiding buttons and loose threads. But an afternoon's sewing is a small price to pay for an enduring place among family memorabilia.

MATERIALS

For a baby's quilt measuring 28in (70cm) × 39in (100cm)

- Red and green check lawn for front squares: ⅔yd (50cm) of 45in (115cm) fabric
- Blue and green check lawn for front squares: ⅔yd (50cm) of 45in (115cm) fabric
- White and red check lawn for front squares: ⅔yd (50cm) of 45in (115cm) fabric
- Red cotton lawn for underside and hearts: 1⅔yd (1.5m) of 36in (90cm) fabric
- Navy cotton lawn for piping: ⅔yd (50cm) of 36in (90cm) fabric
- Piping cord: 4½yd (4m)
- Lightweight wadding: 1yd (90cm) of 45in (115cm) wadding
- Red chenille for outlining hearts: 2½yd (2.25m)
- Paper-backed adhesive web for attaching appliquéd hearts
- Red and navy sewing thread

The Fabrics

Checks, predominantly red, green, blue, and white, machine-quilted onto a rich red underside, and narrowly bound in navy blue.

Quilt front squares

Quilt underside and hearts for squares and corners

Quilt piping

COMPONENTS
Below are the elements needed for a 28in (70cm) × 39in (100cm) quilt

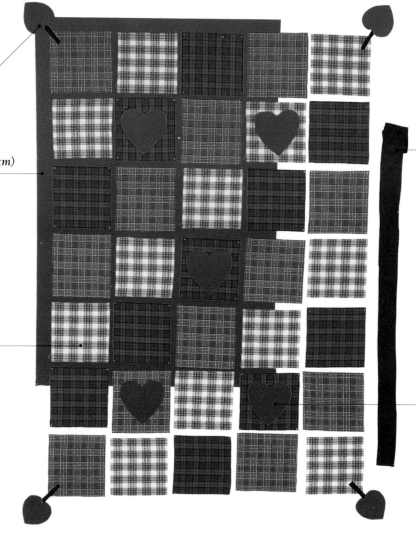

Quilt hearts at corners:
8 hearts (4 with 2 sides each) the size of small template on p. 16

Quilt underside:
29½in (75cm) × 41in (104cm)

Quilt front squares:
35 squares 6½in × 6½in (16.5cm × 16.5cm)

Binding:
2½in (6.25cm) × 142in (361cm)

Quilt hearts on squares:
5 hearts the size of large template on p. 16

Making the Quilt

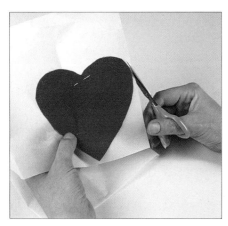

1 Cut out 35 squares following components guide (see p. 10 for multiple cutting techniques). Using the large heart template on p. 16, cut 5 hearts out of the scarlet fabric.

2 Using the same template, cut 5 hearts out of paper-backed adhesive web and iron 1 to the wrong side of each heart.

3 Peel the paper backing from the adhesive web, revealing the adhesive surface.

4 *Iron hearts onto the center of 3 dark, 1 medium, and 1 light tartan square, following the components guide.*

5 *Zigzag stitch hearts onto squares over thick red wool or chenille yarn for extra definition. Pin the wool or yarn in position first for accuracy. You will need about 17in (43cm) of yarn for each heart.*

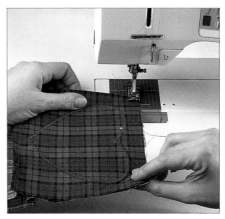

6 *Sew squares together, right sides facing and with a ⅜in (1cm) seam, into strips of 7 squares each. Arrange them following the components photograph. Press seams open.*

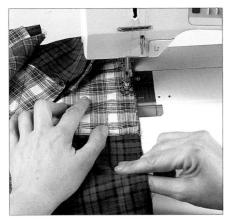

7 *Sew strips together, right sides facing and with a ⅜in (1cm) seam, using the components photograph as a guide. Be careful to match square seams as you proceed.*

8 *Once you have finished the top cover, press it thoroughly, seams open, on the wrong side.*

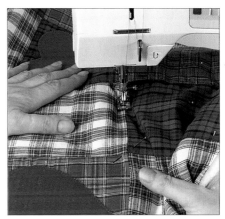

9 *Pin or tack wadding to the back of the quilt. Sew along all seams using straight stitch or zigzag stitch.*

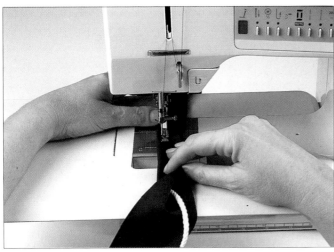

10 *For the piping, cut binding fabric into strips 2½in (6.25cm) wide and join together to make a strip at least 142in (361cm) long (see p. 13 for binding techniques). Press seams of binding open and sew around piping cord using zipper foot and matching dark blue thread (see p. 14 for piping techniques).*

11 *Pin or tack piping in position around edges of quilt top (see p. 14 for piping techniques). Clip corners for ease. Stitch in place using zipper foot, leaving a few inches unsewn at both ends.*

Making the Quilt (cont.)

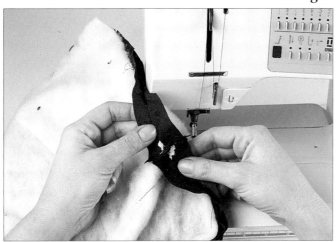

12 *Cut piping cord where it meets and hand sew strips together. Stitch the last few inches to the quilt.*

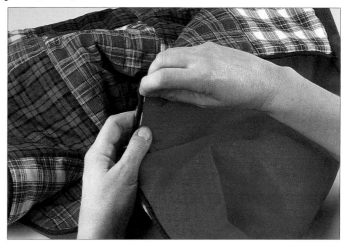

13 *Having attached corner hearts (see step 6 of Making the Hearts), cut quilt underside following components photograph and pin in place being sure to catch top, wadding, and underside. Hem in position by hand, with a seam allowance of ⅜in (1cm).*

Making the Hearts

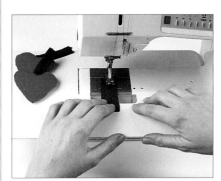

1 *Cut out 8 strips of navy binding, 1½in (3.75cm) wide, 2in (5cm) long. Fold in half lengthwise and hem by machine ¼in (0.5cm) from edge. Turn inside out.*

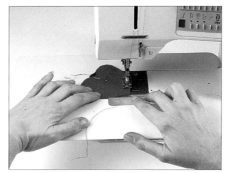

2 *Using the small heart template on p. 16, cut out 8 hearts (see p. 10 for multiple cutting techniques) and pin pairs right sides together with navy strips inside. Stitch around edges, only stitching navy strip in place at the top. Leave a 1in (2.5cm) opening at the bottom.*

3 *After making the hearts, clip the tops carefully up to the seam to make it lie better when it is turned the right side out.*

4 *Turn hearts right side out and stuff the hearts with fluffed-up wadding.*

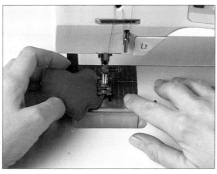

5 *Straight stitch or zigzag stitch around the outside edge.*

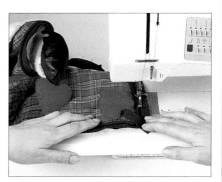

6 *Stitch in place on side of the piping facing the underside. The underside will cover up the ends of the strips when it is hemmed on top of them in step 13.*

Variations

Freehand Flowers

These lively, hand-drawn designs in cool blues achieve a refined look. The underside is a similar print in invigorating red, and the dark blue piping punctuates the edge and links the two sides of the quilt together. An alternative to hearts might be the owner's initials in bold blue appliquéd to the top.

Quilt front squares

Quilt underside

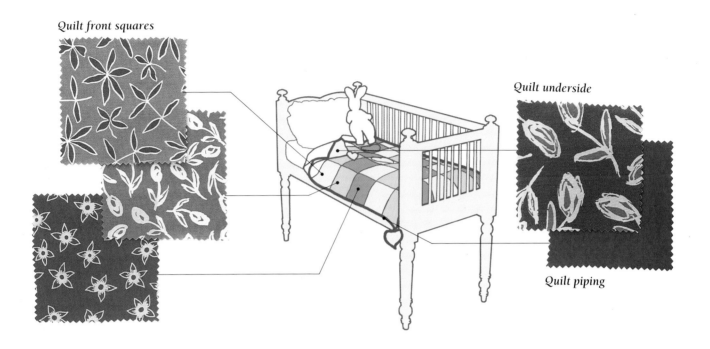

Quilt piping

Honeysuckle and Roses

This enchanting combination of rosebuds and nosegays in shades of pink, white, and gray cotton is lovely for a baby girl's crib. Five honeysuckle sprigs cut from coordinating fabric are appliquéd in place of hearts. The piping is plain pink and the underside candy-striped pink and white sprinkled with roses.

Quilt front squares

Quilt underside

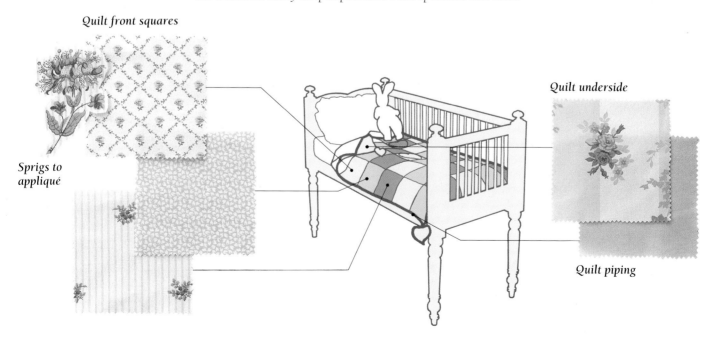

Sprigs to appliqué

Quilt piping

CURTAINS

Seaside Stripe Curtains

*Three variations of blue and white ticking and stripes
combine in a fresh window treatment that recalls the crisp,
clean spirit of a seaside holiday.*

THE SEDUCTIVE CHARM of blue and white has been exploited since Byzantine and Ming potters first used the combination in the fourteenth century. It is one of those infallible partnerships that can do no wrong. The warm off-white of bleached cotton marries perfectly with any blue, but especially the rich cobalt of indigo-dyed cloth which just gets better as it fades and ages. These curtains with their kindred blind have the relaxed good looks of nautical tackle: unfussed simplicity is the keynote here – the three stripes in curtain, blind, and tie-back have impact enough without embellishment. Small details like using a shell instead of a blind-pull, loops instead of curtain heading, and the navy zigzag stitching around the bottom and side hems of the blind, take on real significance. An optional wisp of lace adds a discreet note of softness to counter the otherwise crisp mixture.

These curtains and blind fit in with the simplicity of the wooden walls and floors, giving a breezy, summery feel, but this simple formula works well in endless permutations. Heavy velvet winter curtains in glowing garnet red hung from a mahogany pole and bordered with an antique fringe of slightly tattered gold and ruby chenille will happily partner brocade ties and a silk Ikat blind; plain calico curtains and chambray ties and loops would look well with an indigo blind made from precious cassava resist dyed African Adire cloth; chintz curtains awash with overblown roses could be tied back with a darker chintz in a simpler, coordinating design, and accented with a crisp blind of shirting cotton, finished with chunky cream lace; blue and gold swirls, tied back with a check in matching colors, could be further brightened by a yellow damask shade with a plain blue border along the bottom.

MATERIALS

*For a pair of curtains to fit a
window measuring 38in
(96.5cm) × 56in (142cm),
30in (76cm) from the floor.*

Fabric for curtains: 3yd (2.7m) of
60in (150cm) fabric
White sewing thread
Curtain rod to measure

*For two tie-backs, each
27in (69cm) long*

Fabric for tie-backs: ½yd (46cm)
of 60in (150cm) fabric
Four shells
White sewing thread

*For a blind 38½in (98cm)
× 79in (200cm)*

Stiff cotton fabric: 2¼yd (2.05m)
of 45in (115cm) fabric
Cotton lace: 1¼yd (1.1m) of 2in
(5cm) lace
Navy blue sewing thread
White sewing thread
Roller blind kit to measure
Cord: 1yd (90cm)
Brass hardware for cord
Shell for cord

The Fabrics

*A classic combination of colors that will never fall
from grace – variations on a blue and white theme,
with stripes of different width in close-weave cotton.*

Curtains

Blind

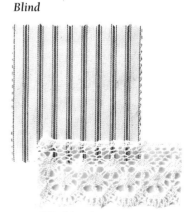

Blind border

Curtain tie-backs

Making the Curtains

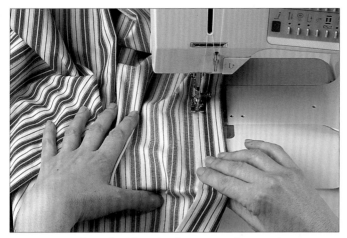

1 *Measure and cut the fabric for the curtains (see p. 8 for measuring techniques), allowing for a 1½in (3.75cm) seam on each side. Cut 2 separate facing strips to the same width and 2½in (6.25cm) deep. Stitch a seam 1½in (3.75cm) wide down both sides of the first curtain.*

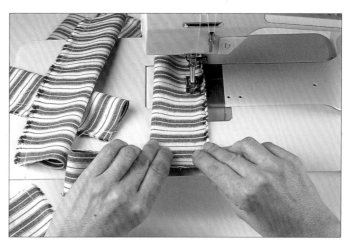

2 *To make curtain loops, cut 12 bands (6 for each curtain) from the same fabric as the curtain, each 5in (12.5cm) wide, 10in (25cm) long. Stitch them into cylinders by folding each in half right sides together, and sewing along their long edges with a ½in (1.25cm) seam allowance.*

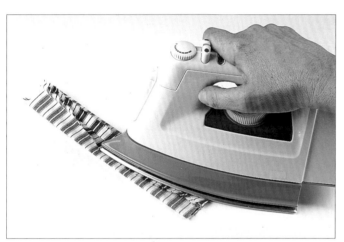

3 *Position each band so that the seam runs down the center and press the seam open.*

4 *Turn the bands right side out and press again along the seam to make sure the seams are lying flat.*

5 *Fold bands in half, seam side inward, and, with the raw edges aligned at the top, pin 1 to the front of each end of the curtain. Measure equidistant positions for the remaining 4 bands (here 8¼in [21cm] apart) and pin them in place.*

6 *Pin facing strip along the top of the curtain right sides together, over the bands. Stitch along the top leaving a ½in (1.25cm) seam allowance.*

7 *Turn facing over to wrong side. Turn it under and pin a ½in (1.25cm) edge along the length and at the ends, maintaining an even depth.*

8 *Stitch along the length and ends of the facing to secure both the facing and the bands to the curtain.*

9 *Turn up and pin a hem to required length (trim excess fabric if hem is more than 6in [15cm]). Stitch down 1 edge of the hem, across the width and up the other edge. The stitches are visible so the line must be straight. Use a line of tacking stitches or a chalk line to guide you if need-ed. Repeat the whole process for second curtain and hang curtains.*

Making the Tie-backs

To make the two tie-backs, cut two strips of fabric, each 9in (23cm) × 60in (150cm). Stitch them into cylinders as in step 2 of *Making the Curtains*, but make sure to leave an unsewn gap of about 6in (15cm) in the middle for turning right side out. Press the seams open as in step 3 of *Making the Curtains* and stitch a shallow "v" (our "v" is 1½in [3.75cm] deep) from the sides to a point in the middle seam at either end. Trim off the excess fabric outside the "v" and turn right side out.

Tease out the points at either end with a knitting needle by pushing outwards from the inside. Press carefully as in step 4 of *Making the Curtains*, turning under the unstitched edges of the long seam, and slipstitch (see p. 11) invisibly together.

To attach the shells, drill a small hole at the end of each of the shells and sew one to the point at each end of the tie-backs. Sew a loop or ring to the center of each tie-back to attach them to a wall hook.

Making the Blind

1 *Measure and cut the fabric for the blind (see pp. 8–10 for measuring and cutting techniques), allowing for a 2in (5cm) hem on each side, 1in (2.5cm) for attaching the blind to the roller, and 2⅛in (5.4cm) for the bottom hem.*

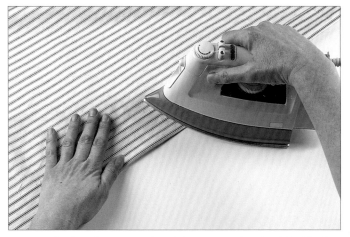

2 *Turn back and press 2in (5cm) hems on each side of the blind. After pressing, pinning is not necessary.*

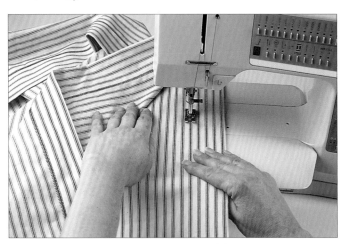

3 *Zigzag stitch down hems in navy blue, following a stripe or pattern if there is one, to keep the stitching line straight. If there is not, mark a guiding line first since the stitching will be visible.*

4 *Along the bottom edge, turn up and pin a 2in (5cm) hem with a ⅛in (4mm) seam allowance and press to provide a crease along what will be the bottom of the blind when the hem is stitched.*

5 *Unpin hem and pin and stitch the straight edge of lace onto the hem side of the crease. This means that when the hem is repinned and stitched, the stitching attaching the lace to the blind will be invisible from the front.*

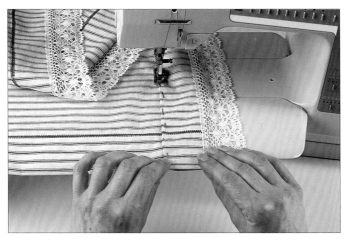

6 *Pin the hem back up and zigzag stitch along its length in navy blue, leaving the ends open to insert the wooden lath. Attach the top of the blind to the roller following the instructions in the kit.*

Variations

Provençal Roses

Surprising, slightly offbeat color combinations are successful when they appear in well coordinated designs such as these for the curtain and tie-back. The curtains would look good very full, possibly draped around the curtain pole. The blind is of crisp, finely striped shirting cotton, finished with chunky cream lace.

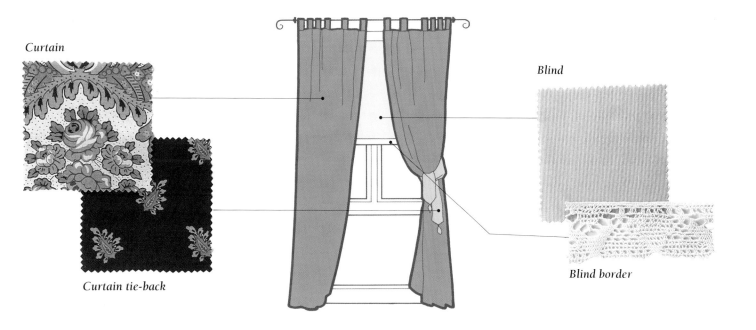

Curtain

Curtain tie-back

Blind

Blind border

Blue and Gold Swirls

With a perfect color match, you can mix the swirling design of the curtain fabric with the checks of the tie-back. On a tall window, you could also use the check for a cornice or hem border to add a crisp finish. The yellow damask blind will always look sunny and is finished neatly with a border of plain blue.

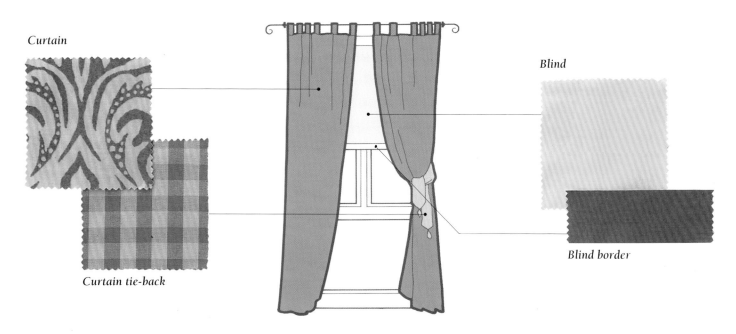

Curtain

Curtain tie-back

Blind

Blind border

Café Curtain

*As simple as can be – sage green and slate blue checks
on hand-woven cotton, distinguished by a scalloped top
and shiny brass rings – this curtain allows the best of both
worlds, all the light you could need and the privacy
you want.*

A S THEIR NAME SUGGESTS, café curtains are designed to cocoon cappucino drinkers in a private haven of warmth and intimacy, letting the world speed by unheeded, and the sun stream in if it will. They are the simplest, most versatile way of letting in light while preserving privacy.

This café curtain fits in perfectly with the casual simplicity of the room. The color of the window frame, sill, and chair rail is picked up in the sage green checks, while the natural cotton color reflects the warm cream of the walls. The decorative scallops along the top of the curtain add extra interest. You should adapt their size according to the pattern of the fabric you choose.

Here the curtain covers slightly more than half the window. Adapt the height according to your needs; higher for more privacy or lower to let in more light.

You can use café curtains in any room in your home. Vary the style and color of the fabric you choose to suit the room for which it is intended. For a kitchen or dining room you could use berry-covered gold cotton or some other pattern with a fruit theme. In a study, striped ticking matching the color of the room would be ideal.

The basic concept of the café curtain is so simple that any fabric – solid or sheer, dark or light, checked, striped, or floral – is perfectly suitable. With café curtains, endless moods and permutations are possible.

MATERIALS
For a café curtain to fit a window measuring 38in (96.5cm) × 56in (142cm)

Coarse hand-woven cotton for curtain: 1½yd (1.4m) of 60in (150cm) fabric
Matching sewing thread
Brass curtain pole with brass rings

The Fabric
Sage green, slate blue, and natural white cotton, enlivened with a narrow stripe of butterscotch brown, echoing the classic colors of Shaker interiors and well-ordered peace and calm.

Curtain

Making the Curtain

1 *Measure and cut out the fabric for curtain (see pp. 8–10 for measuring and cutting techniques), allowing 7in (18cm) in all for top and bottom hems. Fold over 3½in (9cm) at the top of the fabric and press. Using the template on p. 16 or one of your own devising, draw evenly spaced semicircles across folded top of the curtain. Leave at least 1in (2.5cm) between each semicircle and 1¾in (4.5cm) at each end.*

2 *Pin ⅜in (1cm) around the outside of the semicircles and at both ends of facing (leaving ¾in [2cm] seam allowance), to hold facing in place. Stitch around semicircles and at both ends of facing.*

3 *Remove pins and cut out semicircles, leaving a ⅜in (1cm) seam allowance.*

4 *Using sharp embroidery scissors, make small slashes in the seam allowance at 1½in (4cm) intervals, taking care not to cut the stitching.*

5 *Trim the top corners at a 45° angle at both ends of the top hem outside the seam allowance. This will reduce the bulk when the curtain is turned right side out.*

6 *Turn the top hem right side out and tease out the points with a blunt needle. Pin top hem with a ⅜in (1cm) seam allowance and stitch.*

7 *Pin up bottom hem edges to desired length on front side of curtain, with a ⅜in (1cm) seam allowance at the top and a ¾in (2cm) seam allowance at each side. Stitch the sides of the hem, creating a pocket.*

8 Turn bottom hem right side out. Pin ¾in (2cm) hems along both sides of curtain and stitch the hems all the way around.

9 Sew the rings by hand to the back of the semicircle points at the top of the curtain. All that should be visible from the front are the rings themselves.

Variations

Summer Fruit

This berry-covered gold cotton would be a perfect choice for a kitchen or dining-room. Since the fabric is lighter, it would be a good idea to make the curtains somewhat fuller.

Ticking

Ticking is a beautiful, inexpensive, and easy-to-use fabric. In this chic combination of navy and gold, it would be handsome in a study window.

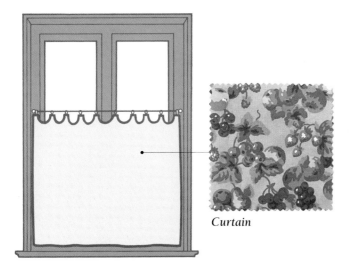

Curtain

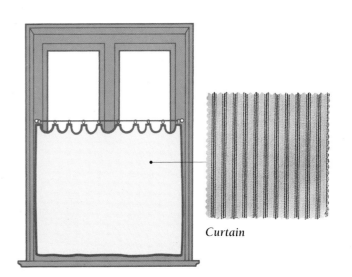

Curtain

Striped Pieced Curtains

Brilliant colors to wake up any décor: three different striped versions of lightweight, woven cotton create dazzling curtains lined in sunshine yellow.

IN GUATEMALA THE HEAT makes the outsized jungle leaves shimmer, and the sun dazzles the eye and bleaches out the hard magenta of the bougainvillaea. Received wisdom is that in such a place bright colors are appropriate, but where ambiguous gray weather predominates, soft colors are right. That is a safe option and discomforts no-one. On the other hand color is a benign magic that can shift mood from dull to sparkling, and strong, vibrant colors bring a defiant surge of optimism and pleasure even on the darkest day.

These generously sized curtains are inspired by the vivid colors of ethnic textiles from Guatemala. They are made from three striped fabrics in different weaves but related tones, which have been joined in deep horizontal bands to add distinction and give a feeling of width to the window. The facing at the bottom acts like a false hem, adding weight to the curtains to ensure that they hang well.

The bright yellow lining is attached to the curtain by two lines of stitching along the top, creating an open pocket through which you slide the curtain pole. The fit around the pole should be tight so that the curtains stay bunched up when pulled back as here, but not so tight that you have difficulty in closing them. Behind the curtain the lining hangs free like a second curtain. The effect, particularly when billowed out by a gust of wind, feels reminiscent of a warm tropical breeze.

The dazzling colors of the Guatemalan fabric are picked up in the bright yellow walls and blue window frame. You should choose your fabric so that its colors and mood fit in with those of the room in which the curtains are to hang. A combination of exuberant cotton prints with charming flora and fauna designs would enliven a child's bedroom, while two fine linens, separated with thinner strips of open-weave braid, would give a more subdued and sophisticated effect.

MATERIALS

For a pair of curtains to fit a window measuring 42in (107cm) × 60in (152cm), 18in (46cm) from the floor.

Striped cotton for narrow strips and facing: 2¼yd (2.05m) of 60in (150cm) fabric
Striped cotton for medium strips: 2¼yd (2.05m) of 60in (150cm) fabric
Striped cotton for broad strips: 2yd (2.13m) of 60in (150cm) fabric
Cotton for lining: 6yd (5.5m) of 60in (150cm) fabric
Matching sewing thread
Curtain pole to measure

The Fabrics

The colors of mango, watermelon, and guava, set off by peacock blue and green in three different fabrics: fine stripes, wide stripes, and an irregular weave laced with plenty of white – an electric mix when combined with the sunshine yellow lining.

Curtain medium strips

Curtain broad strips

Curtain narrow strips

Curtain lining

COMPONENTS

Below are the elements needed for a 46in (117cm) × 87in (221cm) curtain.
Duplicate the components below for the second curtain

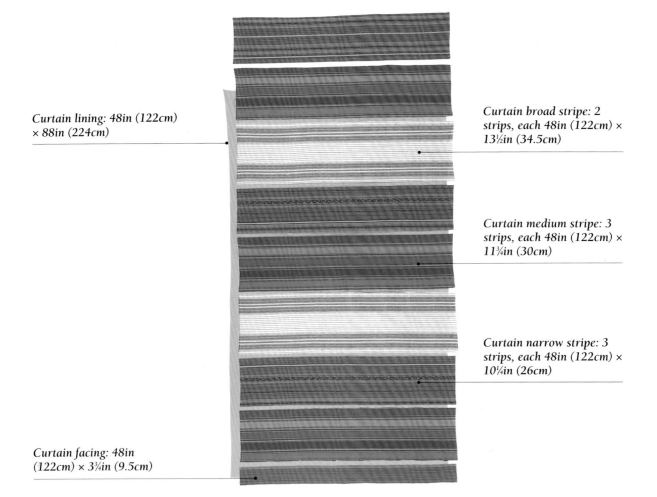

Curtain lining: 48in (122cm) × 88in (224cm)

Curtain broad stripe: 2 strips, each 48in (122cm) × 13½in (34.5cm)

Curtain medium stripe: 3 strips, each 48in (122cm) × 11¾in (30cm)

Curtain narrow stripe: 3 strips, each 48in (122cm) × 10¼in (26cm)

Curtain facing: 48in (122cm) × 3¾in (9.5cm)

Making the Curtains

1 Measure, cut, and lay out all the strips of fabric for both curtains following the components photograph. Having checked that they match each other, pin the strips (but not the facing) right sides together, so every lower strip slightly overlaps the strip above it.

2 Take the fabric for the first curtain and stitch all the strips together, so every lower strip has a seam allowance of ⅜in (1cm) and every upper strip of ½in (1.25cm).

3 *Press all the seams towards the top of the curtain so that the wider seam allowance covers the narrower one. This is so you can stitch flat-fell seams along each strip.*

4 *Turn the edges of the wider seam allowances under the narrower ones and stitch to make flat-fell seams (see p. 12) which should all be ⅜in (1cm) wide.*

5 *Lay the curtain over the lining right sides together, and stitch along the top edge only, with a ⅜in (1cm) seam allowance (the lining hangs free from the curtain at the sides).*

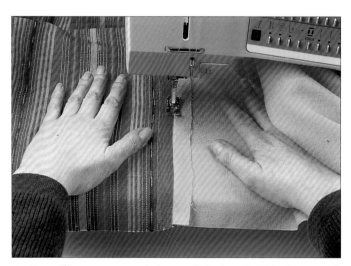

6 *Press the seam open and zigzag stitch along it. This flattens and strengthens the join.*

7 *Pin the facing to the bottom of the curtain right sides together. Stitch it to the curtain along the bottom and at the sides with a ⅜in (1cm) seam allowance, creating a pocket.*

8 *Turn the facing right side out, press it, and pin it to the curtain along the top edge of the facing.*

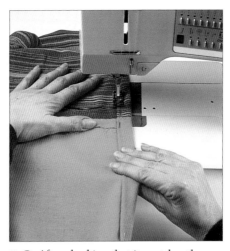

9 *Starting at one of the top corners, pin a ⅜in (1cm) hem and zigzag stitch with yellow thread down the side of the curtain. When you reach the facing, zigzag stitch along it and then go up the other side to the top.*

10 *After checking that it matches the curtain for length, repeat the process for the lining, making a ⅜in (1cm) hem along the sides and bottom.*

11 *Zigzag stitch through the curtain and the lining across the top, leaving a channel wide enough to encircle the curtain pole (see below). Repeat steps 2–11 to make the second curtain.*

Hanging the Curtains

It is essential that the channel at the top of the curtain is exactly the right size for the circumference of the pole. It should be tight enough for the curtains to stay bunched when they are pulled back, but loose enough for the curtains to be easily closed. To achieve this, make the channel about ½ inch (1.25cm) bigger than the circumference of the pole. This pole has a circumference of 3½ inches (8.75cm) so we zigzag stitched 2 inches (5cm) down from the top seam, creating a channel 4 inches (10cm) wide. Ensure that your pole is smooth so that the curtain runs easily along it.

Variations

Birds and Flowers

Exuberant cotton prints of sky-blue and yellow, in charmingly childish flora and fauna designs, are lined with cobalt blue cotton. The curtains would be ideal for a child's bedroom, but could also suit any room hungry for pattern and color.

Curtain broad strips

Curtain narrow strips

Curtain lining

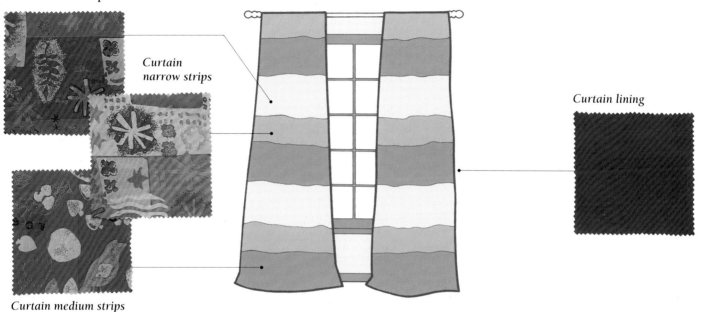

Curtain medium strips

Driftwood Linen

For a different effect, vary the width of the strips. Here open-weave braid separates two transparently fine linens – one in delicate stripes and the other in cleverly woven checks. A cream handkerchief linen for the lining adds to the subtle mixture that would enhance a room with white walls, minimal furnishings, and a floor of bare wooden boards.

Curtain broad strips

Curtain narrow strips

Curtain lining

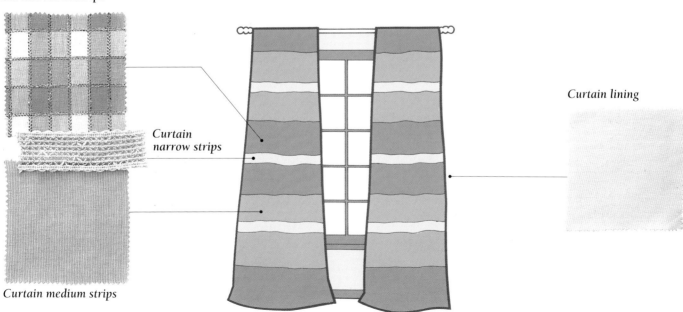

Curtain medium strips

Kilim Print Door Curtain

A heavy, lined door curtain gives a look of baronial splendor to the plainest entrance, and keeps out the draft on wintry evenings.

DOOR CURTAINS ARE a somewhat neglected item, which is a pity since they confer a sense of warmth and grandeur, and make very successful draught-excluders. The size of a door curtain makes it possible to exploit large and dramatic designs such as this heavy cotton with its handsome Turkish rug motif. And, because they are meant to be seen from both sides – particularly if they are to be used as room-dividers or bed-hangings – there is a chance to play with a marriage of contrasting textiles. Here, the red of the ticking picks up the red in the kilim design, and its crisp, formal stripes provide a counterpoint to the rich mixture of pattern and color on the other side.

There are certain considerations to be borne in mind. The curtain should always be at least one-and-a-half times the entire width of the door woodwork. It should easily extend beyond the architraves when drawn and clear the top of the door and moulding by at least an inch

(2.5cm). It is possible to buy curtain rails that attach to the door and open both door and curtain with one single movement, which is a particularly good idea if the curtain is to do duty over a much used door. Their only fault is that they are not usually as good-looking as a straightforward mahogany or wrought-iron pole.

If you do have a simple pole and rings, make sure that the finished curtain does not billow in folds on the floor: it should hang generously so as to exclude draughts, but not be so long that it will catch under the door when it is opened. And it is essential that the rings slide easily along the pole.

Here we have used antique tassels as a tie-back, but, as shown on page 74, you could plait together leftovers of the fabric you use for the curtains.

Once the practicalities have been resolved, there is nothing like a heavy door curtain to give an air of luxury to the most modest entrance.

MATERIALS

For a door curtain to fit a door measuring 81in (206cm) × 36in (91.5cm)

Furnishing cotton for curtain front: 2½yd (2.3m) of 60in (150cm) fabric
Cotton ticking for lining: 2½yd (2.3m) of 60in (150cm) fabric
Wool domette interlining: 3½yd (3.2m) of 45in (115cm) fabric
Herringbone webbing for joining interlining and for pleats: 1¾yd (1.6m) of 2in (5cm) webbing
Matching sewing thread
Curtain rings and rod to measure

For a plaited tie-back measuring 23½in (60cm) long
Furnishing cotton for tie-back: ½yd (46cm) of 60in (150cm) fabric
Cotton ticking for tie-back: ¼yd (23cm) of 60in (150cm) fabric
Kapok stuffing: 8oz (225g)

The Fabrics

Heavy, close-woven furnishing cotton in a glowing kilim design of cinnabar red, slate blue, stone, black, and white contrasts harmoniously with striped cotton ticking.

Curtain front

Curtain lining

Making the Curtain

1 *To join domette interlining, cut a length of webbing to the curtain width (here 59in [150cm] plus 1in [2.5cm] for seam allowances). Place 1 piece of domette along center of tape and zigzag stitch together. Match second piece of domette against first piece and stitch down onto tape in same way.*

2 *Spread domette out flat and, having cut front fabric, lay it on top, right side up. Smooth out creases starting from center and pin the 2 layers together at 8in (20cm) intervals, working outwards from the center in top to bottom rows.*

3 *Cut away any surplus domette interlining at the edges of the front fabric.*

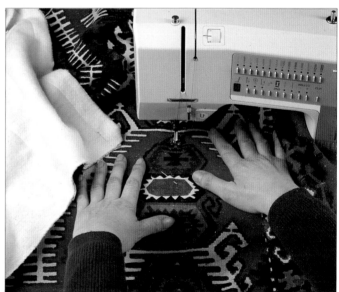

4 *Stitch a quilting line from top to bottom down center of curtain, using the pattern to keep straight. Repeat at no more than 8in (20cm) intervals to the left and right, finishing with a line ½in (1.25cm) from each edge. Use matching thread.*

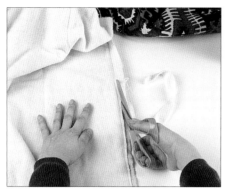

5 *Cut domette back as close as possible to quilting line at each outer edge so that the side seams will be less bulky.*

6 *Cut lining fabric to same length but 1in (2.5cm) narrower than front fabric and pin together along long sides, right sides together. Stitch down long sides ½in (1.25cm) in from edge, leaving about 8in (20cm) unstitched at hem end of seam for adjusting curtain length.*

7 *Pin front and lining fabrics together at top, starting in the center and working out toward both sides. The front fabric will form an edge ¼in (6mm) wide on both sides of lining fabric. Stitch along top ½in (1.25cm) from edge.*

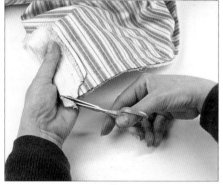

8 *Cut away seam allowance at corners to reduce bulk and give a sharper corner when curtain is turned right side out. Turn curtain right side out.*

9 *Using a tape measure, pin equidistant pleats at top (see p. 14 for pleating techniques). We inserted 5 pleats, each 2in (5cm) wide.*

10 *For hanging the curtain, cut 7 8in (20cm) strips of webbing. Fold them in half and pin against the pleats' inside edge and to the curtain back at each end. Make top of loops level with curtain top.*

11 *Starting 1¼in (3cm) from top of the curtain, stitch a rectangle with crossed diagonal lines to anchor pleat and webbing together. You are stitching through all thicknesses so you should use a strong needle.*

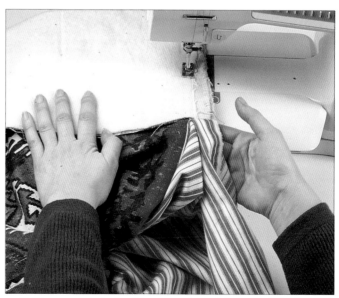

12 *Hang curtain by hooking rings through loops and check length. Pin up sides of front fabric hem accordingly, right sides together, and stitch up both sides ½in (1.25cm) from edge.*

Making the Curtain (cont.)

13 *Cut away corner, turn right side out and pin up hem of front fabric. Sew up by hand with a herringbone stitch (see p. 11) ⅜in (1cm) in from raw edge.*

14 *Pin up lining fabric hem allowance, right sides together, and stitch up both sides ½in (1.25cm) from edge. Cut away corner and turn right side out.*

15 *Pin lining to outer fabric along unstitched sides and bottom and slipstitch together (see p. 11). Hang the curtain.*

Making a Plaited Tie-back

To make the tie-back, first estimate the necessary finished length by looping a measuring tape around the curtain drawn back as you like it (see page 9 for measuring techniques). Add 6in (15cm) to this length for the shortening effect of the stuffing and plaiting. Cut two strips of curtain fabric and one of lining fabric to this length, all 8in (20cm) wide.

Fold each strip right sides together along the longer edge and stitch with a ⅜in (1cm) seam allowance to form narrow tubes. Press the seams open and turn tubes right side out. Positioning seams at center back, stitch across one edge of each tube, ½in (1.25cm) from edge. Fill each with kapok – aim for a soft, even filling.

When tubes are full, stitch across the other ends, ½in (1.25cm) from edge to prevent the kapok from escaping. Stitch the three tubes flat together at one end, making sure the long seams are hidden underneath, and plait them together loosely. Stitch the other ends of the tubes flat together and stitch rings to each end to attach the tie-back to the wall.

Variations

Sumptuous Silks

A dark silk Ikat lined with glowing silk checks would make a beautiful bedhanging. Crisp white bed linen and lace would contrast beautifully with its rich dark colors and you could tie it together by making an eiderdown from matching silks.

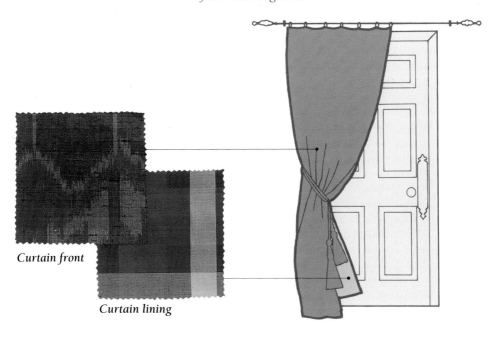

Curtain front

Curtain lining

Stripes and Stars

Floaty cotton voile looks stunning hung in front of French doors. Use the bright transparent stripes on the inside and the tiny gold stars on cream facing the outside. The combination conjures up bright, warm climates, and would look perfect with whitewashed walls, scrubbed wood, and sun streaming in.

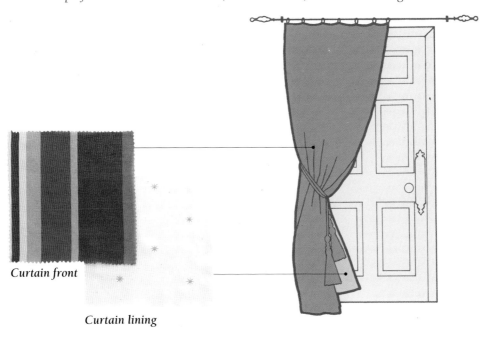

Curtain front

Curtain lining

Pleated Cupboard Curtains

*Rows of tiny cloud-gray stars on soft white cotton chambray
have been pleated to make cupboard curtains that epitomize
the fresh, unpretentious spirit of French country style.*

A MODERN FITTED KITCHEN, crammed with identical pieces of furniture, often lacks character. Kitchens were not always like this. Once, especially in France, the kitchen was the heart of the house and the place where people congregated to gossip, eat, and drink. In the days before everything was sacrificed to an unconsidered obsession with wipe-down and easy-clean, the furniture was functional but it was also pretty. All the culinary apparatus was stored in solid, capacious *armoires de cuisine*, often given a touch of delicacy by a wash of color and a wisp of printed muslin or a waft of very white lace at the doors.

There is something particularly attractive about the contrast between the solidity of wooden furniture and the softness of fabric, and lining cupboard doors like this is an easy way to achieve it. The delicate folds in the fabric set off the hard lines of the furniture and pleating also makes the cotton chambray less transparent.

Fabrics soften the general masculinity of furniture and their use does not have to be confined to the kitchen. Bathrooms and bedrooms can also benefit from an elegant touch of texture and color. You can use sheers or lace, gathered or stretched flat, for the same light, airy look shown here. Darker, solid fabric matched to the paint color or harmonizing with natural wood would look handsome in a more formal setting.

Fixed curtains such as these can be hung using spring rods or plastic coated wire (see page 9). The idea could be adapted for other applications too: sheer drapes on French doors let in light while preserving privacy, and any suitable fabric can be attached to hinged wooden frames to make a room divider screen.

MATERIALS

All curtains to fit a cupboard with two windows measuring 12in (30cm) × 34in (86cm)

For two pleated curtains:
Cotton muslin for curtains: 2¼yd (2m) of 45in (115cm) fabric
White sewing thread
Curtain hardware (see p. 9)

For two flat curtains:
Close-weave cotton for curtains: 1¼yd (1.15m) of 45in (115cm) fabric
Matching sewing thread
Curtain hardware (see p. 9)

For two gathered curtains:
Cotton voile for curtains: 2¼yd (2m) of 45in (115cm) fabric
White sewing thread
Curtain hardware (see p. 9)

For two pleated and tufted curtains:
Cotton muslin for curtains: 2¼yd (2m) of 45in (115cm) fabric
Silk embroidery yarn
White sewing thread
Curtain hardware (see p. 9)

The Fabric
Subdued gray-blue stars subtly dot delicate white cotton voile.

Curtain

Making Pleated Curtains

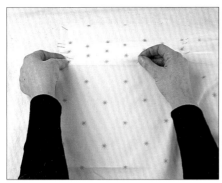

1 Measure and cut a piece of fabric 2¾in (7cm) longer than the height of the cupboard opening and 3 times the width. Pleat and pin it (see p. 14 for pleating techniques) at regular intervals straight onto an ironing board cover (here we make ½in [1.25cm] wide pleats).

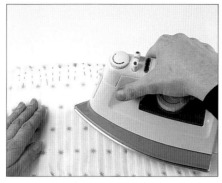

2 Having pulled the pleats straight and ensured both ends are even, press the pleats in position.

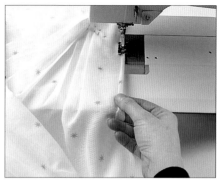

3 Check that the pleated curtain is at least 2in (5cm) wider than the cupboard and stitch a ¼in (6mm) wide hem down each side. Stitch at both ends to keep the pleats in place.

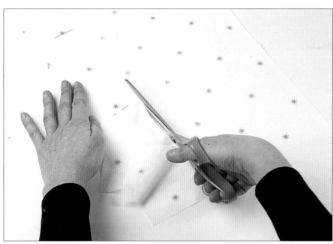

4 To secure the pleats and create channels for curtain rods, cut 2 strips of fabric 3½in (9cm) wide and 2in (5cm) longer than the width of the cupboard opening. Before cutting, use pins to ensure that the design is in the same position on each strip.

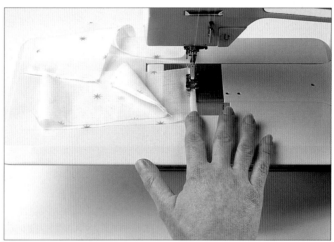

5 Make a ¼in (6mm) hem at the ends of each strip. The strips should now be the same length as the width of the pleated curtains.

6 Pin and tack a strip along the top of the curtain right sides together (the hems of the strip should be facing outwards), making sure the pleats remain flat.

7 Stitch the pleated curtain to the strip from the back of the curtain with a ⅜in (1cm) seam allowance, and remove the pins and tacking.

8 *Zigzag stitch along the seam edge from the front to prevent the open weave material from fraying.*

9 *Turn and pin the strip onto the wrong side of the curtain tucking under a ⅜in (1cm) hem. Stitch carefully along the hem and repeat the process from step 6 for attaching second strip to bottom of curtain. Repeat entire process for second curtain. See p. 9 for techniques on hanging cupboard curtains.*

Curtain Styles

The simplest cupboard curtain of all (near right) exploits a beautiful, medium weight cotton which is just stretched over the cupboard opening. Cut a piece of fabric to the depth of the opening plus 5in (12.5cm) for hems and channels for rods, and the width of the opening plus 2in (5cm) for side hems.

Another alternative is voile, here printed with mulberry red heraldic animals. It gathers beautifully into a translucent curtain which hints at the cupboard's contents while concealing the clutter. To achieve the gathering effect shown here, you need a piece of fabric 3 times wider than the cupboard opening, plus the normal allowances for sides and for seams. In place of voile, you could use other delicate fabrics such as lace or net, which would both be particularly suitable in a bedroom.

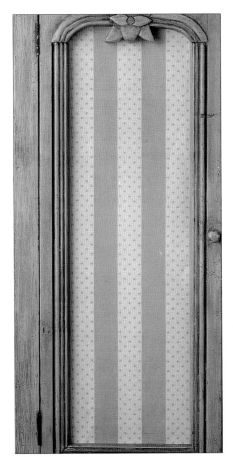

Making a Tufted Curtain

You can pull together a tricky color scheme by customizing your fabric with matching tufts. Here we have used silk embroidery yarn, but you could also use fine satin ribbons tied into tiny bows on a more open weave fabric, giving the curtain a feminine look, or shells, beads, or pearls for textural interest.

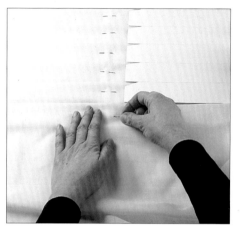

1 *Using a sheet of cardboard at least the width of the cupboard opening as a template, mark it with parallel lines 2in (5cm) apart. Cut out a triangle at the end of each line as shown and use it as a guide for pinning and stitching the pleats (see p. 14 for pleating techniques and step 1 on p. 78).*

2 *Using a ruler for accuracy, mark where you want the tassels to go. Here we have created a diamond pattern by inserting them on alternate pleats in rows across. Cut equal lengths of the yarn and then thread them through from the front, one color at a time as shown. Check that protruding strands are equal in length and knot them together. Follow steps 2–9 of Making Pleated Curtains (pp. 78–79) to finish off.*

Variations

Blue Spots

Regular spots on slightly uneven woven cotton voile would look pretty gathered and used in a painted or polished wood country cupboard.

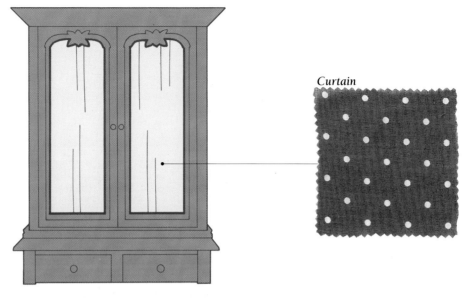

Curtain

Pink Flowers

Nosegays of pink flowers on cotton muslin would suit a feminine bedroom. Use them for matching dressing-table skirts or swags.

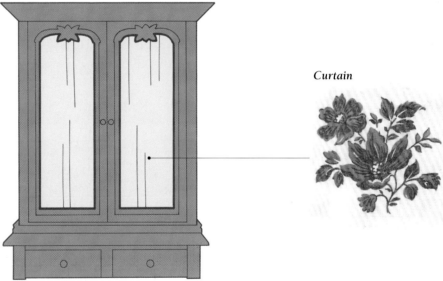

Curtain

Gold Lions

Winged lions among the stars printed on cotton voile would look splendid gathered or pleated in a dining-room sideboard cupboard, hiding shelves of white crockery.

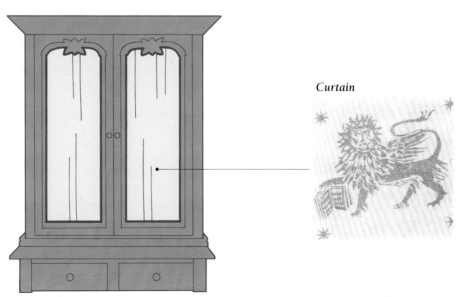

Curtain

SEATING

Bench Cushion

Colonial Cushions

Patchwork Wool Cushion

Striped Satin Cushion

Woolen Throw

Bench Cushion

A color combination of crisp denim blue, red, and white stripes tied with bright red tape brings a welcome touch of comfort to a spartan seat.

SOLID RECTANGULAR CUSHIONS, often referred to as squab cushions, serve a multitude of purposes. They can make a window seat into a cosy retreat, add comfort to the seat-numbing hardness of garden furniture, and make a fireside settle, charming but unyielding, into a less penitential place to roost.

Our cushion cover exploits the harmonious partnership between coordinating, close-woven, denim-weight cottons. When you come across a family of fabrics like this, it is an irresistible challenge to find a place for them, because they always look good together and someone else has done all the work of matching and balancing. So your task remains the simple enjoyable one of choosing the designs you like, deciding which shall go where and what trimmings to use. Here, the bright red of the bows picks up the thin red stripe in the fabric used for the inside cushion and the same bright red has been used for the piping around the two complementary cushions.

The cover inside a cover is an effective design that is very simple to make. It has a casual air which can be smartened up by using a grander selection of fabrics – sitting-room window seats might aspire to tapestry fabric in soft restrained colors, with matching plain silk for the inside cover. It can be further dressed up with additional matching cushions or a pair of bolsters or matching curtains. Alternatively, you could choose a bright-colored print of sunflowers in washable cotton to bring a bench cushion in your kitchen to life.

MATERIALS

For a bench cushion 13in (33cm) × 37in (94cm) × 2⅜in (6cm)

Striped denim for outer cushion: 1⅓yd (1.2m) of 45in (115cm) fabric
Striped denim for inner cushion: 1⅓yd (1.2m) of 45in (115cm) fabric
Cotton tape for ties: 2¾yd (2.5m) of 1in (2.5cm) tape
Red and navy blue thread
Zip: 1yd (90cm)
Foam rubber cushion pad: 37in (94cm) × 13in (33cm) × 2⅜in (6cm)

For 2 accompanying cushions 16½in (42cm) square

Striped denim for cushions: 20in (50cm) of 45in (115cm) fabric for each cushion
Cotton tape for piping: 4½yd (4m) of 1in (2.5cm) tape
Piping cord: 4½yd (4m)
Matching sewing thread
Two feather-filled cushion pads: 16½in (42cm) square

The Fabrics

Indigo blue and wine red on a natural cotton ground, here spiced up with the scarlet red of the bows, is an association of colors that never fails in a combination of different stripes.

Cushion

Outside cushion

Inside cushion

Cushion

Cushion bow and piping for cushions

Making the Cushion

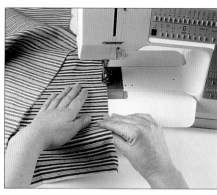

2 *Zigzag stitch along all the raw edges to prevent the fabric from fraying.*

1 *For the outer cover, measure and cut out fabric to required size. To do this, fold fabric in half lengthwise to width of cushion and add 4in (10cm) for seam allowances plus the cushion pad depth. To determine fabric length, add ¾in (2cm) for seam allowances plus twice the cushion pad depth to the required length.*

3 *Fold fabric in half lengthwise, right sides facing, and stitch along side seams, with ⅜in (1cm) seam allowance. Press seams open.*

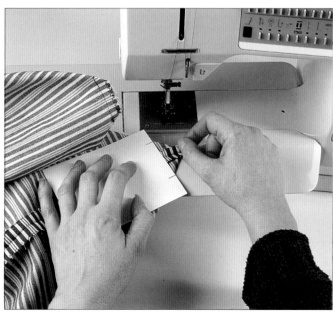

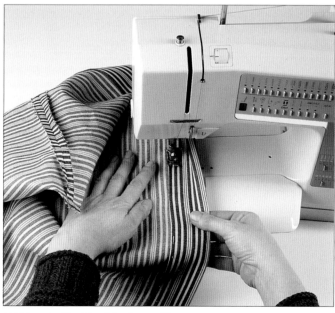

4 *Mark a piece of cardboard to match the cushion depth and place it diagonally across the opened-out corners. Stitch across the corners to create a box shape and trim corners to reduce bulk.*

5 *Turn in 2in (5cm) for hem of front opening. Pin in position and stitch all the way around.*

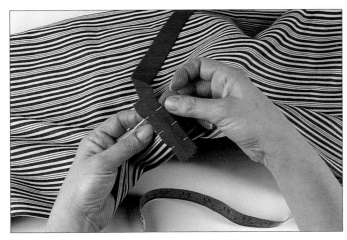

6 To make ties, cut 4 pieces of tape to desired length (here each is 21in [53cm] outside the cushion plus 2in [5cm] inside). Pin 2 pieces to hem of one side of cushion (here, pieces are 11in [28cm] in from seam on both sides). Pin other 2 pieces to hem in matching positions on the other side of the cushion.

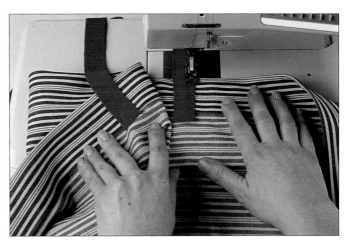

7 Attach tapes by stitching a rectangle and crossing inside it diagonally for added strength. Hem other end of tape by hand to prevent fraying.

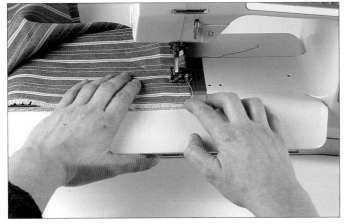

8 Cut out fabric for inner cushion. Fabric length is the same as outer cover, but, after folding in half lengthwise to width, add 1in (2.5cm) for seam allowances plus twice the depth of cushion pad. Zigzag stitch along all raw edges, fold fabric in half length-wise, right sides together, and stitch a seam 2½in (6.25cm) long at one end, with a ½in (1.25cm) seam allowance for zip opening.

9 Press open seam and ½in (1.25cm) seam allowance for zip. Starting at the stitched end, pin and tack open zip in place on top of pressed seam allowance.

10 Turn the fabric right side out and stitch the zip in place along both edges, using the zipper foot. Make sure pressed edges meet exactly. Turn wrong side out and stitch remaining seam allowance at other end of zip. Press open seam.

11 Lay cover down so back seam with zip is centered and then pin, stitch, and press open the 2 end seams, with ⅜in (1cm) seam allowance. Ensure that the zip is partially open so the cover can be turned right side out after stitching. Remove tacking stitches along zip, turn right side out, and insert cushion pad.

Making Complementary Cushions

Both of these cushions are made in exactly the same way. For each cushion, cut a piece of fabric 17½in (44.5cm) square and two pieces 13in (33.5cm) × 17½in (44.5cm). Make sure that the stripes on the second two pieces go the same way and that each has a 17½in (44.5cm) side cut along a selvage if possible. Turn each selvage inside and stitch a ¾in (2cm) hem.

Lay the two rectangles on top of one another with the hemmed edges towards the middle and the right side of one facing the wrong side of the other. Adjust their position until between them they form a 17½in (44.5cm) square (they should overlap by approximately 7in [18cm], forming a flap for the cushion opening). Pin and stitch these pieces in position.

Make 70in (180cm) of piping for each cushion by stitching the red binding around the piping cord using a zipper foot (see page 14 for piping techniques).

Place front of cushion on top of back, right sides facing, and check that the stripes match and are going in the same direction. Pin and tack front and back together with piping sandwiched in the middle (see below). Clip piping corners to assist turning. Stitch around edge and zigzag along all raw edges to prevent fraying. Turn right side out and press.

Repeat entire process for second cushion and insert cushion pads.

Variations

Antique Tapestry

A medieval flower design in soft tapestry colors would make an inviting window seat. Plain silks for the inside cushion and accompanying cushions pull out colors from the design. You could also make accompanying curtains in the same color or fabric.

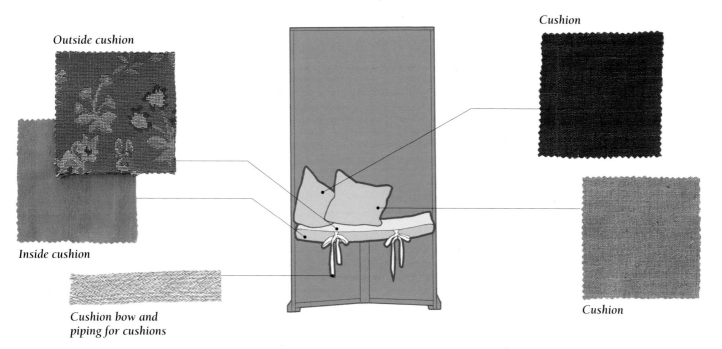

Outside cushion

Cushion

Inside cushion

Cushion

Cushion bow and
piping for cushions

Country Kitchen

Bold sunflowers on washable cotton perfectly color-matched with a tiny farmyard print makes a whimsical combination for a bench cushion in a bustling kitchen. Green ties bring out the green in both prints, and green is echoed again in piping around cushions of red and yellow.

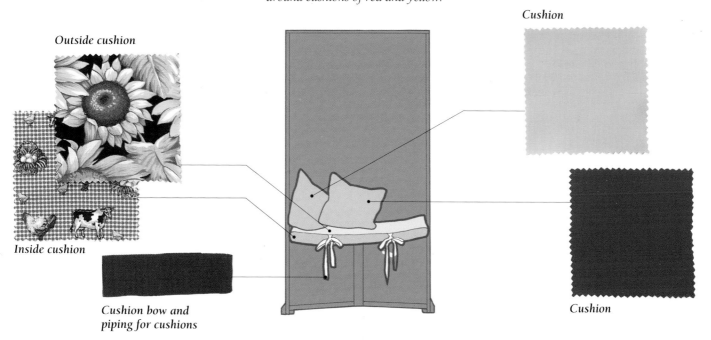

Outside cushion

Cushion

Inside cushion

Cushion

Cushion bow and
piping for cushions

Colonial Cushions

A seductive nest of cushions piled into a wicker chair, in variations on a red and white theme. A simple lace insertion is accompanied by traditional American embroidery, Flying Geese patchwork, and the plainest of piecing.

ONE OF THE EASIEST WAYS to bring warmth to a room is with an inviting pile of cushions. They add color and cheer, and contribute softness, luxury and comfort at a fraction of the cost of new upholstery and decoration. Mixing and matching color and texture is an endless source of creative fun – taking color cues from paint or furniture and harmonizing with darker or brighter, printed or plain.

In this instance, a dignified interior with painted matchboard walls, wide plank flooring and a capacious wicker chair is brought to life by accents of crisp red and white, picking up the red in the antique Boston rag rug. A collection of different fabrics and designs, linked by color, provides richness and variety. Checks, stripes, patchwork and embroidery work beautifully together.

Of course, when choosing colors you can use a wider palette. You could enjoy coordinating tapestry colors, using varying shades of one color, or playing different patterns and colors against each other. Having chosen your color scheme, you can proceed to haunt the remnants counter in your favorite fabric store and snap up any lengths of trimming or tassel that might be appropriate. A little embellishment can make a lot of difference and a gold-stenciled or appliquéd heraldic motif, an edging of braid, or corners weighted with chunky tassels can transform the common cushion into something exotic and sumptuous.

Visible closures such as the bows used on the gingham and stripes cushion are a decorative alternative to conventional zips or snaps, and offer another means of embellishing your cushions. As for other decorations such as appliqué, embroidery, or stenciled motifs, the only limit is your imagination. Cushions are a good place to begin experimenting with fabric, since if the worst comes to the worst and the fabric just will not behave, you will not have bankrupted yourself.

Lace Insertion Cushion

MATERIALS
For a lace insertion cushion 16in (41cm) square

Linen for cushion cover: ½yd (46cm) of 45in (115cm) fabric
Cotton insertion lace: 1⅓yd (1.22m) of 2¼in (5.7cm) lace
Cotton for cushion lining: ½yd (46cm) of 45in (115cm) fabric
Matching sewing thread
Two ¾in (2cm) white buttons
Feather-filled cushion pad: 16in (41cm) square

The Fabrics
A cheerful combination of red and white in a classic strip contrast of heavy white linen and delicate insertion lace, set off nicely by the strong red of the lining.

Cushion lining

Cushion cover

Cushion insertion lace

COMPONENTS

Below are the elements needed for a 16in (41cm) square cushion

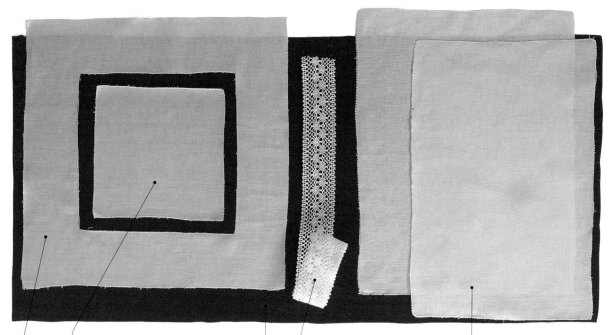

Cushion cover front center: 7½in (19cm) square (to be trimmed to fit exactly later)

Cushion cover front border: 16¾in (43cm) square with a 8¾in (22cm) square cut out of its center leaving an even 4in (10cm) border.

Cushion insertion lace: 2¼in (5.7cm) wide × 1¼yd (1.1m)

Cushion lining: 16¾in (43cm) × 36¾in (94cm)

Cushion cover back: one piece 10½in (27cm) × 16¾in (43cm); one piece 13in (33cm) × 16¾in (43cm)

Making the Cushion

1 *Having cut out the fabric for the cushion following the components photograph, zigzag stitch around all raw edges to prevent fraying. Press a ¼in (6mm) seam allowance around inside of the back of the border, cutting at corners to make it lie flat.*

2 *Turn border over to right side and, starting at a corner, pin lace around inside of border, just overlapping the seam allowance. Fold over the lace on the back side at corners as shown. Stitch from back following the pins, taking care not to catch the folded lace at the corners.*

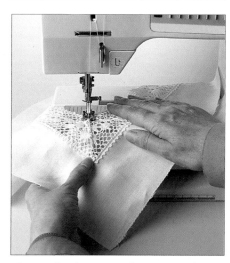

3 *Turn border over and zigzag stitch twice (⅛in [3mm] apart) across the corners of the lace diagonally. Pull the threads to the back and knot.*

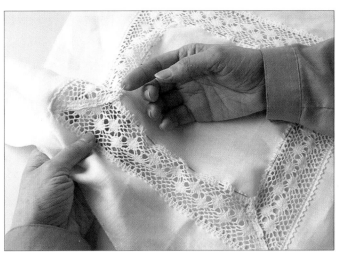

4 Trim away surplus folded lace at the corners on the back, being careful not to cut through the stitching.

5 Trim center square to fit, allowing for a ¼in (6mm) seam. Press seam (cutting at corners) and pin center in position so lace just overlaps seam. Stitch close to selvage of lace.

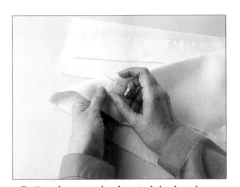

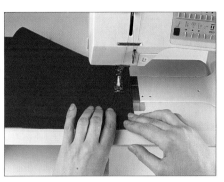

6 For the cover back, stitch by hand or machine a 2in (5cm) hem along 1 longer side of both the back pieces. If the side is a selvage you need not turn the fabric under.

7 Pin the two back pieces so that the hems overlap and then pin cover front to back, right sides together. Stitch front and back together and zigzag ¼in (6mm) in from raw edges. Turn right side out and press. For directions on making buttonholes and sewing buttons see pp. 14 and 29.

8 To make lining cushion, cut out fabric following components photograph and stitch a ⅜in (1cm) hem at both ends. Fold over one end by 4in (10cm) and stitch up sides to make a pocket. Fold in half, right sides together, and pin and stitch a ⅜in (1cm) seam down both sides. Turn right side out and insert cushion pad, closing by pulling pocket flap over, like a sandwich bag.

Variation

Medieval Bestiary

A forest green lining adds richness to a quaintly charming cotton print of animal woodcuts in soft green, brown, and cream. The simple cotton insertion lace adds to the general air of antiquity.

Cushion cover

Cushion lining

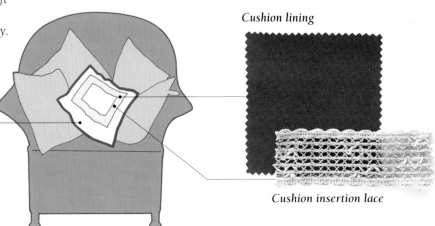

Cushion insertion lace

Embroidered Good Morning Cushion

To make the cushion, cut out the fabric following the measurements below. Use dressmaker's carbon paper to transfer the embroidery template on page 19 to the center of the front cover and stem stitch (see page 11) the design. Stitch a 2in (5cm) hem, with ⅜in (1cm) turned under, on one of the longer sides of both back pieces. Pin the two back pieces with the hemmed edges towards the middle and adjust their position until between them they form a 16½in (42cm) square (they should overlap by approximately 3½in [9cm]). Pin front to back, right sides together. Stitch, with ⅝in (1.5cm) seam allowance, and trim corners. Turn right side out, press, and stitch all around 1in (2.5cm) from outer edge.

MATERIALS

Homespun cotton for cover: ½yd (46cm) of 45in (115cm) fabric
Matching sewing thread
Standard embroidery thread
Dressmaker's carbon paper for transferring template (see page 19)
Button: ¾in (2cm)
Feather-filled cushion pad: 13⅜in (34cm) square

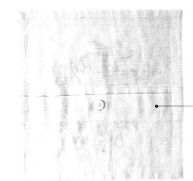

Cushion back: one piece 16½in (42cm) × 12½in (31cm); one piece 16½in (42cm) × 11¼in (28.5cm)

Cushion front: 16½in (42cm) square

Flying Geese Cushion

To make the cushion, cut out the fabric following the measurements below (see page 10 for multiple cutting techniques). Stitch small triangles to large triangles to make 21 rectangles and stitch them together to make three strips of seven (see directions for *Making the Flying Geese Quilt*, steps 1–5 on page 39 for technique). Pin and stitch flying geese strips to 4 shorter front divider strips, right sides together and with a ⅜in (1cm) seam allowance. This should be done in such a way that the flying geese strips and divider strips alternate, with a divider strip on either edge. Stitch on the two longer divider strips top and bottom, right sides together and with a ⅜in (1cm) seam allowance, and press all seams open. For the cushion back, make a ¾in (2cm) hem on the longer edge of both pieces. Fold 2 strips for ties in half, wrong sides together, turn in seams and stitch to make ties. Stitch one tie to the center of the hemmed edge of the larger back piece. Stitch the other tie in the center of the other back piece, 3⅛in (8cm) in from the hem. Pin the back pieces so that they overlap in the middle, matching the size of the front, and pin to the front, right sides facing. Stitch front to back with a ⅜in (1cm) seam allowance and turn right side out. Press and insert cushion pad.

Cushion back: one strip 16½in (42cm) × 9½in (24cm); one strip 16½in (42cm) × 11½in (29cm)

MATERIALS

Checked cotton for cushion back and cushion front divider strips: ½ yd (46cm) of 45in (115cm) fabric.
Large triangles for cushion front: ½yd (45cm) of 45in (115cm) fabric in total
Small triangles: ½yd (45cm) of 45in (115cm) fabric
Matching sewing thread
Feather-filled cushion pad: 15¾in (40cm) square

Cushion front divider strips: four strips, each 2⅛in (5.5cm) × 15⅜in (39cm); two strips, each 2⅛in (5.5cm) × 16⅞in (43cm)

Cushion front large triangles: 21 right-angled triangles in 3 coordinating patterns (see template on p. 15)

Cushion front small triangles: 42 right-angled triangles (see template on p. 15)

Cushion back ties: two strips, each 1¼in (3cm) × 11¾in (30cm)

Red Mitered Cushion

To make the cushion, mark and cut out fabric following the measurements given. Cut diagonal edges and pin, stitch, and press the cushion front borders in same way as with *Provençal Tablecloth* (page 112, steps 2–3), but attach pieces right sides together instead of wrong sides together. Attach the center panel as with *Provençal Tablecloth* (page 113, steps 4–6) but again attach pieces right sides together instead of wrong sides together. For the cushion back, make a ¼in (6mm) hem along 1 long side of both strips. Fold loop strips in half, wrong sides together, and stitch with a narrow turning. Fold these in half make loops and stitch them to the back of one of the hems, spacing them evenly. Pin back strips together with a 3⅛in (8cm) overlap and pin to cover front, right sides together. Stitch around edges with a ⅜in (1cm) seam allowance. Turn right side out and sew on buttons (see page 14). Press and insert pad.

MATERIALS
Wide checked gingham for front: ⅓yd (30cm) of 45in (115cm) fabric
Striped cotton for front and back: ½yd (46cm) of 45in (115cm) fabric
Matching sewing thread
Two ¾in (2cm) buttons
Feather-filled cushion pad: 15¾in (40cm) square

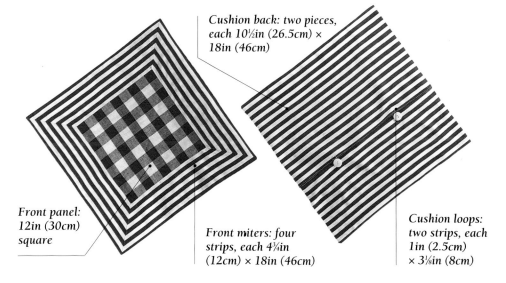

Cushion back: two pieces, each 10½in (26.5cm) × 18in (46cm)

Front panel: 12in (30cm) square

Front miters: four strips, each 4¾in (12cm) × 18in (46cm)

Cushion loops: two strips, each 1in (2.5cm) × 3⅛in (8cm)

Bow-Tied Gingham and Stripes Cushion

To make the cushion, cut out the fabric following the measurements given. Fold ties in half widthwise, wrong sides together, and stitch to make ties, folding under raw edges (see page 14 for techniques on making ties). Make a ⅜in (1cm) hem along one of the shorter sides of the cushion front and sew front cover ties to outside of hem, spacing them equidistant from each other and the cushion front edges. Turn over hemmed edge by 2¾in (7cm), wrong sides together. Stitch sides, making a pocket. Sew cushion back ties in corresponding positions on cushion back as those on cushion front, 2¾in (7cm) from selvage. Pin front to back, right sides together (with ties and facing on outside), and stitch around edges with a ⅜in (1cm) seam allowance. Fold over opening seam allowance corners 45° and stitch to neaten. Turn right side out and press.

MATERIALS
Gingham for front and ties: ½yd (46cm) of 45in (115cm) fabric
Striped cotton for back and ties: ½yd (46cm) of 45in (115cm) fabric
Matching sewing thread
Feather cushion pad: 15¾in (40cm) square

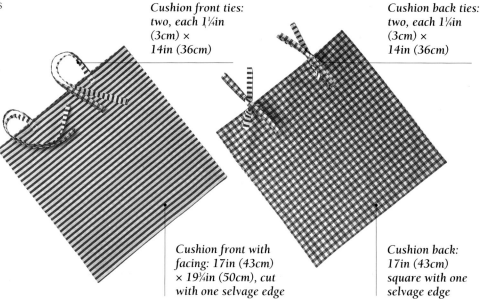

Cushion front ties: two, each 1¼in (3cm) × 14in (36cm)

Cushion back ties: two, each 1¼in (3cm) × 14in (36cm)

Cushion front with facing: 17in (43cm) × 19¾in (50cm), cut with one selvage edge

Cushion back: 17in (43cm) square with one selvage edge

Patchwork Wool Cushion

A textured tweed cushion with a shaggy fringe offers a soft haven of warmth and comfort perfect for a winter evening spent in a leather armchair by the fireplace.

WINTER CALLS FOR a radical rethinking of furnishings and fabrics. Floral linen, cotton checks and tiny prints in bright colors are right for summer when doors and windows are wide open and you can bid outdoors in. But when the evenings lengthen and there is a chill in the air, when the retreat into squashy armchairs and cosy sofas is imminent, something different is called for. Nothing beats warm wools and tweeds for instant insulation.

As the fabric changes, so should the colors. The warm chestnut and russets of bare bark and autumn leaves and the rich, dark brown of Jacob sheep come into their own and prove perfect companions for ancient kilims and polished furniture.

Before you start, make sure your cushion pad is in good condition. Throw out any that have lost their shape and substance and invest in new ones. Down or feathers fill a cushion more luxuriously than synthetic fibers, which soon become lumpy and stiff. Always measure your cushion pad carefully so that your finished cover fits snugly. Underfilled cushions seem old and tired.

The cushion shown here is a simple combination: patches of subtly colored Harris tweed alternating with a bold cream and brown check, accentuated by the deep beige fringe and the corduroy backing.

The dark, subdued colors fit in well with the rich browns of the table and chair, and the squares tie in perfectly with the checked wallpaper.

MATERIALS
For a cushion 22in (56cm) square

Harris tweed for front squares:
⅓yd (30cm) of 45in (115cm) fabric
Checked tweed for front squares:
¼yd (23cm) of 45in (115cm) fabric
Fine-wale corduroy for back: ⅔yd (61cm) of 45in (115cm) fabric
Natural cotton rug fringing for fringe: 2½yd (2.25m)
Zip: 20in (51cm)
Matching sewing thread
Feather-filled cushion pad: 22in (56cm) square

The Fabrics
A checkerboard of classic wool – peat brown Harris tweed enlivened with a hint of unexpected green and fox red, contrasting with a bold cream and brown check discreetly etched with blue.

Cushion back

Cushion front squares

Cushion front squares

Cushion fringe

COMPONENTS

Below are the elements needed for a 22in (56cm) square cushion

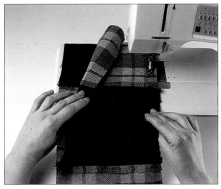

Harris tweed cushion front squares: 5 squares, each 8½in (21.5cm) square

Checked tweed cushion front squares: 4 squares, each 8½in (21.5cm) square

Cushion back: 2 pieces, each 12in (30.5cm) × 23in (58.5cm)

Cushion fringe: 2½ yd (2.25m)

Making the Cushion

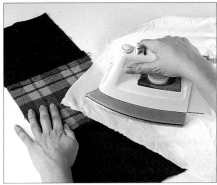

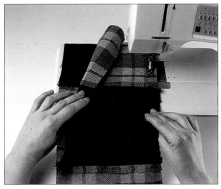

1 Using the components photograph as a guide for size and pattern, cut, pin, and stitch the front squares right sides together into three strips, with a ½in (1.25cm) seam allowance (see p. 10 for multiple cutting techniques).

2 Press seams open from wrong side, using a damp cloth to protect the wool.

3 Again using the components photograph as a pattern guide, pin and stitch 2 strips right sides together, with a ½in (1.25cm) seam allowance. Check pattern is correct and attach third strip in same way. Press seams as before.

4 Starting in the center of one edge, tack a continuous piece of fringe to cushion front, right sides together, with the fringe's seam pointing outwards. Match ends of fringe edging together and overstitch as shown above.

5 Slash fringe edging at the corners so that edging will lie flat when stitched.

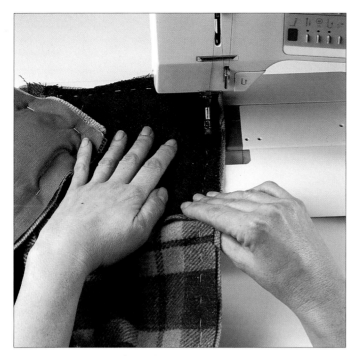

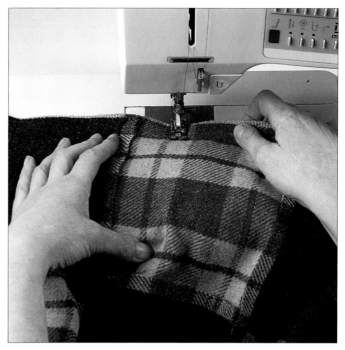

6 *Having cut pieces for cushion back following components photograph and inserted zip following instructions for Striped Satin Cushion (steps 1–2, p. 102), pin back and front right sides together. Using zipper foot, stitch around cushion through all layers with a ½in (1.25cm) seam allowance.*

7 *Overstitch ends of fringe edging within seam allowance to strengthen it and prevent fraying. Turn right side out and insert cushion pad.*

Variation

Autumn Colors

Guatemalan woven cotton in rich, earthy colors paired with coarse cotton in bright pumpkin make a cheerful checkerboard. The piping is natural herringbone braid and the back is close-woven cotton with tan and conifer green stripes.

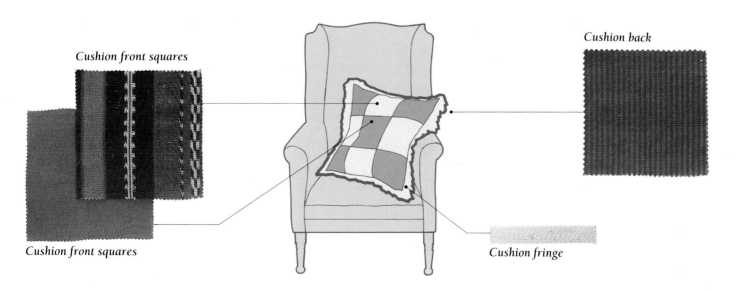

Cushion front squares

Cushion back

Cushion front squares

Cushion fringe

Striped Satin Cushion

A simple shape given exotic treatment in sumptuous satins.
Braid and tassels, the crisp definition of black piping, and a
burgundy and black version of the fabric for the back produce
a mood of Far Eastern opulence.

ROMANCE AND DRAMA are as important in life as good sense and washability. A hint of decadence, an echo of the Casbah, the rich and vibrant colors of Moorish interiors, of such things are dreams made. Bedroom or boudoir is the place for fantasy, a tasselled satin cushion the least that Mata Hari or Rudolf Valentino would expect.

One of the pleasures of soft furnishings is that they do not have to be expensive or even permanent. Cushions are the furnishing equivalent of jewelry – the perfect way to emphasize and underline a color scheme. They pick up or contrast tone and pattern, and act as necessary interest and punctuation in a plain interior.

Cushions can be designed to match mood or season: this glorious and extravagant conjunction of fabrics and colors is perfect for a boldly theatrical interior and quick to make besides. The broad lines of black braid isolate the bright woven satin stripes of the center panel from the more delicate stripes of the border fabric. The braid accentuates the striped design and links in with the black piping around the edge. A single cushion looks good, and a pile of them in slightly different weaves and shades would be spectacular.

While your budget may not allow the use of costly fabrics on a large scale, cushions such as this one provide an opportunity to use velvet, brocade, or silk left over from dressmaking or bought as remnants. Antique textiles such as small tapestry panels, or a piece of needlepoint you have stitched but do not know how to display, can similarly be shown off to advantage.

MATERIALS

**For a cushion 16½in (42cm) ×
23½in (60cm)**

Striped satin for cushion front
center: ⅔yd (60cm) of 45in
(115cm) fabric
Striped satin for cushion front
borders: ⅔yd (60cm) of 45in
(115cm) fabric
Braid for cushion front divisions:
1yd (92cm) of 1¼in (3cm) braid
Striped satin for cushion back:
¾yd (70cm) of 45in (115cm)
fabric
Ready-made black piping: 2¾yd
(2.5m)
Ready-made red and black tassels
Zip: 22in (55cm)
Matching sewing thread
Feather-filled cushion pad: 23½in
(60cm) × 16½in (42cm)

The Fabrics

*Two stripes in fine satin on the front, woven in distinctive
golds, reds, whites, and black, are set off handsomely by
the subtler dark red and black stripe on the back.*

Cushion front center

Cushion front borders

*Cushion front
divisions and piping*

Cushion back

100

COMPONENTS

Below are the elements needed for a 23½in (60cm) × 16½in (42cm) cushion

Cushion front borders:
2 pieces, each 6½in
(16.5cm) wide, 17¼in
(44cm) long

Cushion front center:
12¾in (33cm) wide,
17¼in (44cm) long

Cushion back: 2 pieces, each 9⅛in
(23.25cm) wide, 24¼in (62cm) long

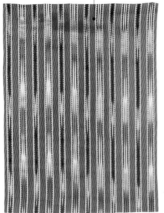

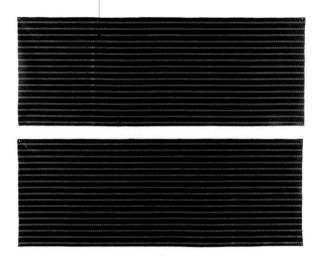

Cushion front divisions: 1¼in (3cm) × 36in (92cm),
cut in half to make two strips 18in (46cm) long

Piping: 2¾yd (2.5m)

Making the Cushion

1 *Cut out fabric following components photograph and pin 2 back pieces right sides together along long edge. Place the zip next to the edge, equidistant from either end, and pin. Stitch a ½in (1.25cm) seam from each end to the zip, overstitching inner end of seams strongly. Open out wrong side up and press open small seams and ½in (1.25cm) seam allowance for zip (see p. 14 for zip techniques).*

2 *Turn right side up and, holding the zip in place at the back, pin it from the right side. Make sure pressed edges meet exactly. Using zipper foot, stitch around zip in 1 stage.*

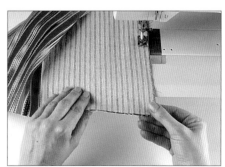

3 *Using components photograph as a guide, join the 3 pieces of fabric for front by pinning right sides together and stitching down the two seams, with ⅜in (1cm) seam allowances. Press seams open on wrong side.*

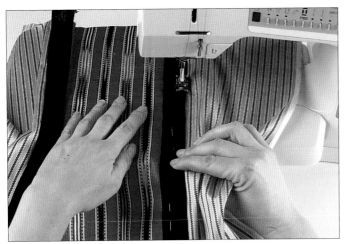

4 With fabric right side up, pin braid in position over center of seams (if braid is stretchy, tack instead of pinning), leaving a ⅜in (1cm) overhang at either end to be trimmed later. Stitch along edges of each piece of braid.

5 Leaving zip partially open, pin front and back right sides together, with ready-made piping in between (see p. 14 for piping techniques), its seam allowance facing outwards. Leave 1in (2.5cm) piping spare at zip seam. Starting at zip seam, use zipper foot to stitch around edge of cushion with a ⅜in (1cm) seam allowance. Leave corners unstitched for insertion of tassels.

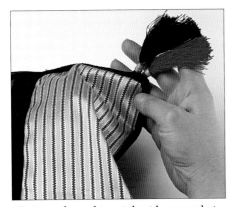

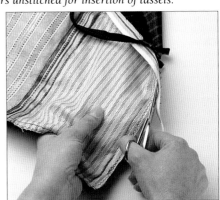

6 Turn the cushion right side out and pin the ends of tassels into the corners which have been left open. Be sure tassels are all the same length.

7 Turn the cushion wrong side out and sew in the tassels and the corners by hand, using double thread. Snip into the seam allowance of the piping cord at the corner so that piping lies flat when it is stitched.

8 Zigzag stitch around the edge of the seam to prevent fraying and trim away any surplus fabric, braid, and piping cord. Turn cushion right side out and insert cushion pad.

Variation

Discreet Stripes

Raw silk in wide stripes of cream and caramel brown, divided by matching lightly flecked braid creates a cool, unfussy look.

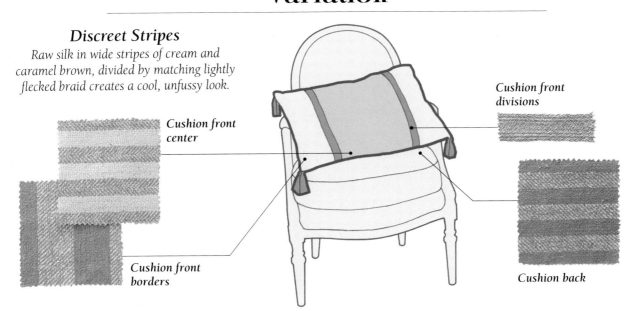

Cushion front center

Cushion front divisions

Cushion front borders

Cushion back

Woolen Throw

An all-purpose blanket-cum-comforter, this luxurious,
warm woolen throw adds old-world style and elegance to the
plainest chair or sofa.

CASUAL ELEGANCE IS what distinguishes the most patrician *palazzo* – nothing fussy, nothing shoddy, just a few good things displayed with panache. The kindly adaptable throw is essential for this kind of grandly spartan life – to soften the crisp exactitude of upholstery, to bring comfort and warmth to a misty winter in Venice, to wrap about the knees in draughty libraries, or around the shoulders for a private post-prandial snooze. Once you have acquired the taste, you will feel that no sitting-room or bedroom is quite furnished without at least one softly draped rectangle of touchable fabric neatly finished – your sofa will suddenly look naked, your fire-side chair impoverished without its winter throw of thick wool.

This is the decorating equivalent of the silk scarf, the ultimate accessory that pulls everything together, or adds a vital punctuation mark or touch of color. Like a scarf, a throw can be used formally and neatly, folded or piled if you have a plethora of them. Or, it can be thrown in inviting *déshabille* over a prim button-back chair.

Color and texture are the things to go for: it must be soft to the touch and drape well. The throw is a sensuous item that should invite you to wrap youself up in it or should drape casually over a chair or sofa for all to admire its rich colors and graceful folds. It can be huge or manageable. It can be bright or subtle, plain or patterned. A throw is just an excuse for enjoyment and can be used to revitalize old, worn upholstery at low cost.

We have made ours from soft reversible wool bound in checked tweed. The dark colors suggest winter evenings by the fire, eating crumpets and reading the latest best-seller, with soothing music in the background.

MATERIALS
For a throw measuring
65in (165cm) × 72in (183cm)

Reversible wool for throw: 2yd
(1.8m) of 80in (200cm) fabric
Checked wool for binding: 1¼yd
(1m) of 60in (150cm) fabric
Navy and camel sewing thread

The Fabrics
Thick, soft wool in reversible camel and navy, bound
neatly in tobacco brown and navy check tweed,
enlivened by a subtle streak of cinnabar red.

Reversible fabric
for throw

Throw binding

Making the Throw

1 For the binding, cut out strips 5¼in (13.25cm) wide (see p. 13 for binding techniques). Join the strips together, matching tweed, so that you have 2 strips at least 70in (178cm) long and 2 at least 80in (200cm) long. Press joined seams flat, using a damp cloth to protect the wool.

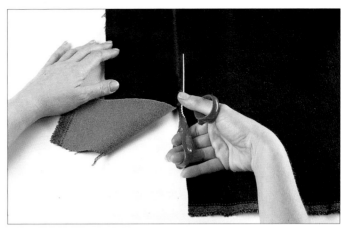

2 Using a carpenter's square and tailor's chalk, mark the reversible fabric to the size you want and cut along the chalk lines. Here we have made a rectangle measuring 65in (165cm) × 70in (178cm).

3 Pin and stitch binding along edges of one side of rectangle, leaving a few inches unstitched before each corner and enough binding to shape miter. Cut, pin, and sew miters in position as shown, leaving ½in (1.25cm) open at each end of miter seam and overstitching there (see p. 12 for mitering techniques).

4 Having pressed the miter seam open, pin the ½in (1.25cm) openings precisely at the corners and complete the stitching of the binding to the throw (see p. 12 for mitering techniques).

5 Turn right side out and press and pin under hem on unstitched edge of binding to meet stitched line.

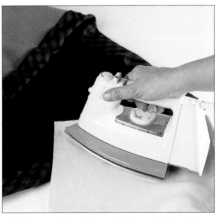

6 Press with a damp cloth, guiding the hem into place with your fingers as you go.

7 Slipstitch the reverse-side hem by hand and press again to eliminate pin marks.

Throw Edgings

Different edge finishes suit different fabrics: fray tapestry to reveal its rainbow warp; finish blanket wool with a classic blanket stitch (see p. 10); fray and knot coarse hand-woven silk tweed (see below).

1 *Remove crosswise threads one at a time to create 3in (7.5cm) of fringe.*

2 *Taking a ⅜in (1cm) section of fringe at a time, make a loose knot and tighten it down to the woven fabric.*

Variations

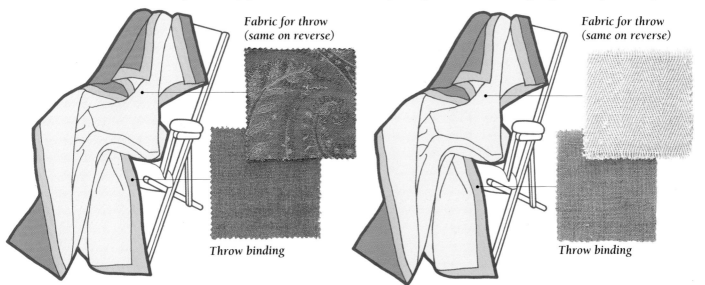

Subtle Paisley
Great swirls of blue paisley tapestry fabric in wool and cotton, bound with terracotta silk, make a sophisticated throw that would be at home in simple or richly patterned interiors.

Fabric for throw (same on reverse)

Throw binding

Summer Naturals
Heavy herringbone weave cream cotton from India bound with unbleached linen scrim, make the perfect summer throw to soften a garden bench or bring elegance to upholstered furniture.

Fabric for throw (same on reverse)

Throw binding

TABLECLOTHS AND BAGS

Provençal Table Linen

Quilted Tote Bag

Picnic Tablecloth and Bag

Provençal Table Linen

*A set of table linen brimming with Mediterranean
exuberance. Bold, bright colors and intricate patterns perfectly
evoke summer in the south of France.*

THERE ARE SOME FABRICS that capture the very essence of the culture that created them, and Provençal cotton is a glorious example. The delicate designs began life in India, as part of an ancient tradition of block printing. The rich colors of the Midi hit this refined tradition like a bolt of electricity, and a brilliant, inimitable fabric was born, redolent of the South of France: terracotta, ochre, and all the colors of sun-parched soil; every kind of marine blue; the yellows of sand, ripe wheat, and sunflowers; the greens of pine and aromatic herbs; the unabashed reds and pinks of poppies, oleanders, and bougainvillaea.

Faced with this cornucopia of color, the natural Northern reaction is to back away and search nervously for cool blue checks and soothing neutrals. This is an impulse to be resisted – such things are excellent in their place, but gray skies cry out to be countered with a defiant dash of sunny color. The truism is that bright shades are all very well in hot climates, but just don't work beyond the maquis. The truth is that bright shades always work – not everywhere and for all uses, but as an unfailing anti-depressant and an occasional and judicious tonic to enliven more restrained color schemes.

The secret of using Provençal fabrics is to exploit the range of harmonizing colors, matching up the contrasting elements and drawing together the different variants of shade and pattern using one of many border designs. The colors need not match exactly (in fact a more lively effect comes from using related but not matching tones) but they should come from the same color family.

MATERIALS

To fit a 27½in (70cm) diameter table

Center: 1¼yd (1.15m) of 45in (115cm) fabric
Insertion: 4yd (3.5m) of 3½in (9cm) fabric
Border: 1¾yd (1.6m) of 45in (115cm) fabric
Binding: 2¼yd (2m) of 60in (150cm) fabric
Underskirt: 4½yd (4.12m) of 45in (115cm) fabric or, if available, 2¼yd (2m) of fabric at least 81in (205cm) wide
Matching sewing thread

For two napkins

Center: ⅔yd (60cm) of 45in (115cm) fabric
Binding: 1½yd (1.3m) of 45in (115cm) fabric
Matching sewing thread

The Fabrics
A vibrant partnership of strong colors – saffron, red, and dark pine green – harmonized by a floral border that reflects the main colors.

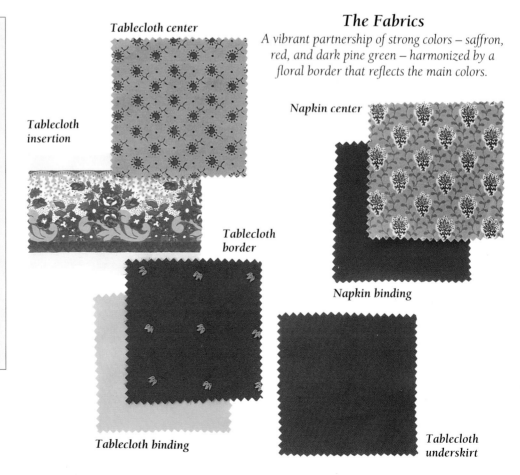

Tablecloth center

Tablecloth insertion

Napkin center

Tablecloth border

Napkin binding

Tablecloth binding

Tablecloth underskirt

COMPONENTS

Below are the elements needed for a 50in (127cm) square tablecloth

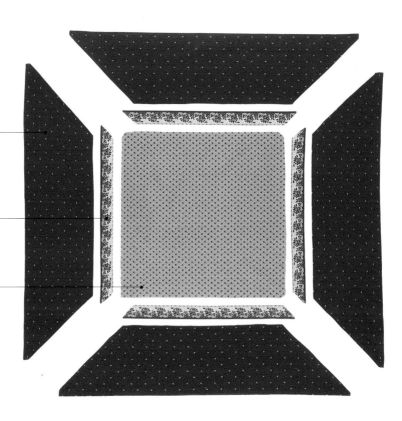

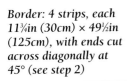

Border: 4 strips, each
11¾in (30cm) × 49½in
(125cm), with ends cut
across diagonally at
45° (see step 2)

Insertion: 4 strips, each
3½in (9cm) × 30in
(76cm)

Center panel: 28⅜in
(72cm) square

Binding: 4 strips, each
2¼in (6cm) wide, at
least 20in (51cm) long

Underskirt:
81in (205cm)
square

Making the Tablecloth

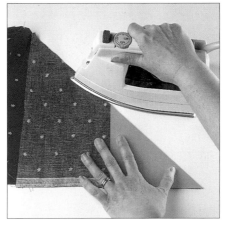

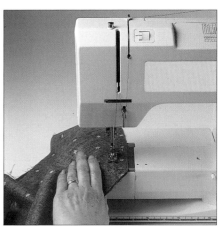

1 Mark and cut the fabric for the insertion and border (see step 2 for cutting the border strips) using the components photograph as a guide and following the pattern, not the weave, of the fabric.

2 To make the diagonal ends on the borders, fold over and press the ends as above, using a 45° template as a guide. Place the shorter side of each border against a side of the center panel to check they are the same length and cut along the fold.

3 Pin and stitch the 4 border strips right sides together along the diagonal ends, with a ⅜in (1cm) seam allowance and stopping ⅜in (1cm) short of the inside corners (see p. 12 for mitering techniques). Draw thread through to back and knot.

4 Place the border over the center panel fabric, aligning the patterns. Mark where they meet with tailor's chalk on the right side of the center panel, allowing for a ½in (1.25cm) seam allowance. Cut out center panel along marked lines.

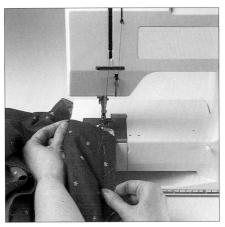

5 Tack and stitch border to center panel wrong sides together, with a ½in (1.25cm) seam allowance. Leave the mitered corners open (see p. 12 for mitering techniques).

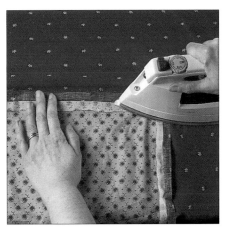

6 Press open the seam on the right side, trimming any surplus fabric at the corners.

7 Place insertion strips centrally over pressed seams. Mark, press, and cut miters (see p. 12 for mitering techniques), allowing for a ⅜in (1cm) seam at corners.

8 Press under seam allowances on both sides of insertion so they can be appliquéd straight onto the tablecloth.

9 Stitch miters of insertion right sides together, leaving inside and outside seam allowances open. Draw thread through to back and knot. Trim outside corners of miter to reduce bulk.

10 Lay tablecloth on flat surface. Starting at corners, pin insertion centrally over pressed seams of border and center panel, following the pattern and matching up the miters. Stitch carefully, ⅛in (3mm) in, along the inside and outside edges of insertion.

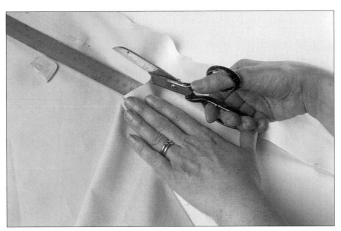

11 Cut and join binding fabric (see p. 13 for binding techniques) to make 4 strips of binding, each 2¼in (6cm) wide, at least 50in (127cm) long. Press ⅜in (1cm) seam allowances on both sides.

Making the Tablecloth (cont.)

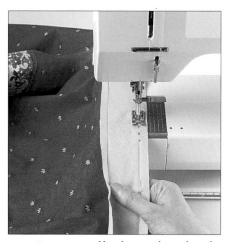

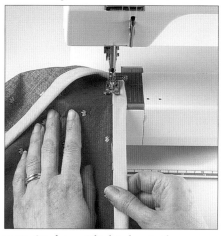

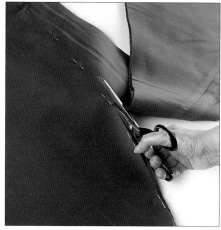

12 *Pin a strip of binding to the right side of 2 opposite border edges and stitch along pressed seam. Fold over and press, tucking under the other seam allowance and ensuring that the binding is at least ⅛in (3mm) wider on the underside.*

13 *Stitch in a "ditch" close to the seam on the top side of the binding, ensuring that you catch the underside of the binding easily. Repeat for other 2 border edges, turning under excess at corners and stitching by hand (see p. 13 for techniques on stitching corners). Press thoroughly.*

14 *For the underskirt, fold and press fabric in half twice and then fold it in half diagonally to form a triangle. Draw a segment of an arc using a pencil fastened to a tack with string (see p. 10 for techniques on cutting a circle). Pin around arc and cut through all layers of fabric. Open out and stitch a narrow hem all around.*

Making the Napkins

To make two napkins, mark and cut two 20in (51cm) squares of the center fabric, following the pattern, not the weave of the fabric. Cut and join binding fabric (see page 13 for binding techniques) to make 8 strips of binding, each at least 20½in (52cm) long, 2¼in (6cm) wide. Press ⅜in (1cm) seam allowances on both sides of each binding strip and attach binding to napkin following the instructions for attaching binding to the tablecloth above (steps 12–13).

Variations

Autumn Russets

*Lively printed and plain cottons in bright terracottas and hyacinth
blue combine to make a tablecloth and napkins ideal for the natural country
look – white walls, seagrass matting, a log fire, and comfortable armchairs
slipcovered in linen.*

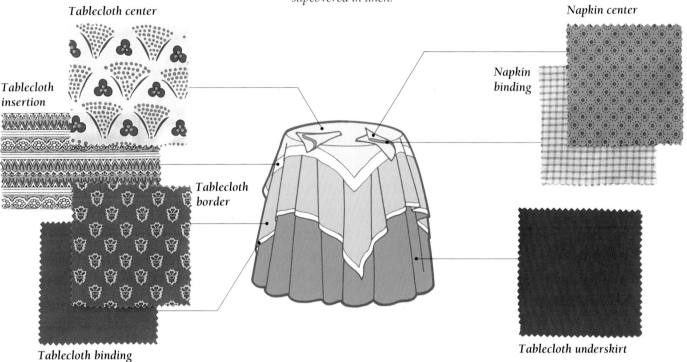

Tablecloth center

Napkin center

Napkin binding

Tablecloth insertion

Tablecloth border

Tablecloth binding

Tablecloth underskirt

Rainbow Linens

*Fine linen dyed in strong, plain colors is combined here with an
underskirt in Guatemalan stripes.*

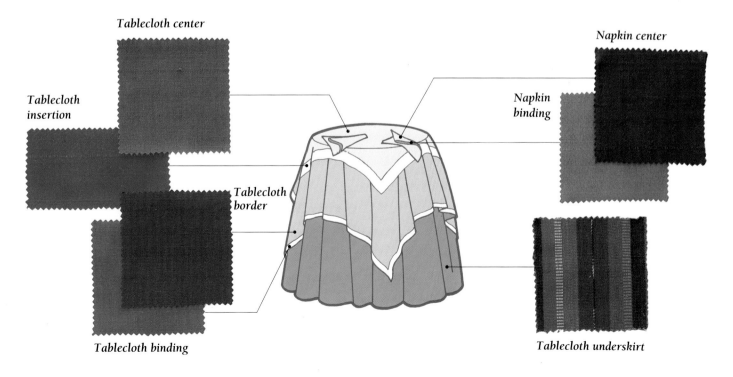

Tablecloth center

Napkin center

Napkin binding

Tablecloth insertion

Tablecloth border

Tablecloth binding

Tablecloth underskirt

Quilted Tote Bag

Warm, muted sunshine colors in a trio of fabrics make a handsome, all-purpose holdall for storing all kinds of clutter.

UNLESS YOU HAVE ESCHEWED material things, you will probably find your home full of bits and pieces for which no space exists, those temporary things that will be cleared up eventually but create devastation in the meantime – like needlework in progress. The solution is a handsome tote bag, which, from cutting out to completion, should be only an afternoon's work.

Once this simple sleight of hand has transformed your life, you will discover that there is a myriad of other uses for good-looking, portable, washable totes. Big ones can tame a spare duvet or sleeping bag that otherwise spills out from its eyrie in the airing cupboard; little ones can house nappies and baby accessories; medium-sized ones can hold your collection of fabric scraps for that patchwork quilt you are going to make one day.

The trio of fabrics used for this bag combine for a warm, muted effect, while the thick, undyed cotton rope, threaded through metal eyelets and finished with large twine tassels you can make yourself, gives the bag a natural look.

In place of these you could use any number of different colored and patterned fabrics, harmonizing them with the room in which the bag will live. Indeed, using the same construction principles, you can adapt the bag's size and shape to your own needs.

MATERIALS
For a bag with a 39in (100cm) circumference, 39in (100cm) deep

Thick cotton for bag outside: 1¼yd (1.15m) of 45in (115cm) fabric
Thick cotton for bag lining: 1¼yd (1.15m) of 45in (115cm) fabric
Thick cotton for binding and base: ½yd (46cm) of 45in (115cm) fabric
Lightweight wadding: 1⅔yd (1.5m) of 45in (115cm) fabric
Knitting cotton for tassels: 1 skein
Natural cotton rope: 3¼yd (3m)
Metal eyelets: 8
Matching sewing thread

The Fabrics
Thick cotton in harmonizing stripes and plaid, in shades of rich, golden yellow, soft smoky gray-blue, dusty brick red, and bleached wood.

Bag outside

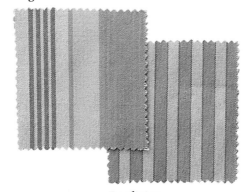

Bag lining

Bag binding and base

COMPONENTS

Below are the elements needed for a bag with a 39in (100cm)
circumference, 39in (100cm) deep

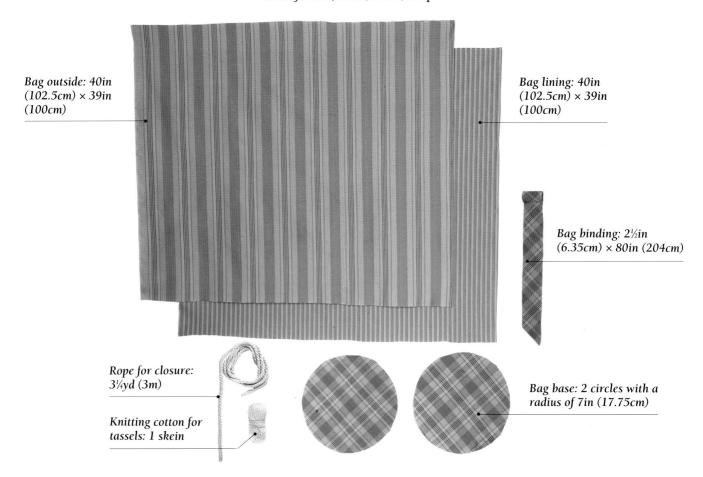

Bag outside: 40in
(102.5cm) × 39in
(100cm)

Bag lining: 40in
(102.5cm) × 39in
(100cm)

Bag binding: 2½in
(6.35cm) × 80in (204cm)

Rope for closure:
3¼yd (3m)

Knitting cotton for
tassels: 1 skein

Bag base: 2 circles with a
radius of 7in (17.75cm)

Making the Bag

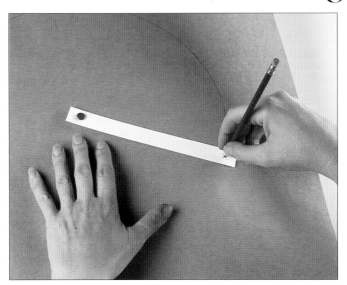

1 Make a template for the base by tacking a sheet of paper at least 16in (40cm) square to a work table. Tack a narrow strip of cardboard 8in (20cm) long to the center of the paper and make a tiny hole at the other end of the card 7in (17.75cm) from the tack to insert pencil. Slowly spin pencil in strip to draw a circle. Cut it out.

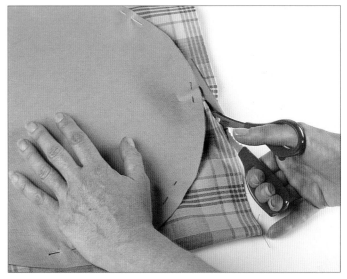

2 For the base, pin the circle to a doubled piece of fabric to cut out 2 circles at once. If you are using a large check like the one shown, ensure that the circle is centered on the pattern.

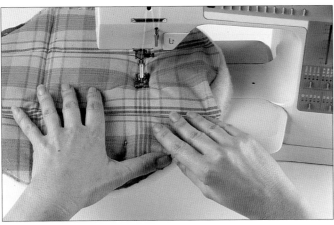

3 Use template to cut out wadding to the same size as the circles and pin the 3 layers together with the wadding in the middle. Stitch 2 evenly spaced quilting lines in both directions across base, making a square in the center.

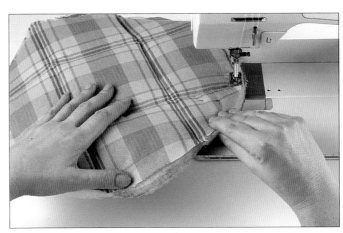

4 Stitch around edge of the base with ⅛in (3mm) seam allowance to keep layers together. Trim excess wadding.

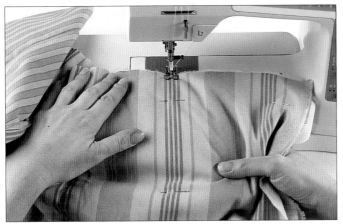

5 Cut out fabric for bag outside and lining following components photograph and cut a piece of wadding to same size. Pin outside, wadding, and lining together 2in (5cm) in from 1 edge from top to bottom. Work across fabric, pinning lines at 5in (13cm) intervals (for quilting lines) until you reach the far edge. Stitch lines from top to bottom.

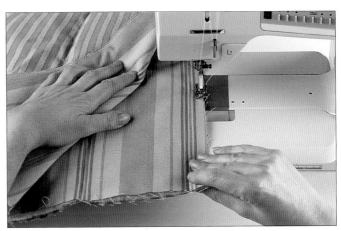

6 Trim any excess wadding from bag edges and zigzag stitch down raw edges on both sides of bag to neaten.

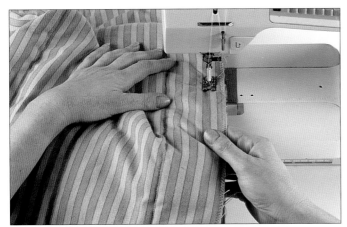

7 Fold bag in half, right sides together, and stitch to make a cylinder with a ½in (1.25cm) seam allowance.

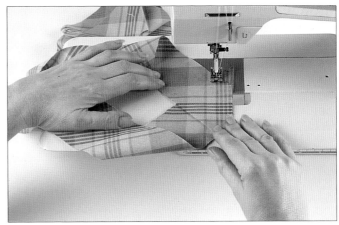

8 Cut and join binding to make 2 strips, each at least 40in (102cm) long, to edge top and base of bag (see p. 13 for binding techniques). If using check as here, be careful to match the checks when stitching strips together.

Making the bag (cont.)

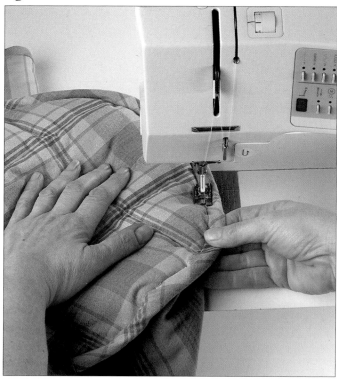

9 Pin and tack bag sides to base, wrong sides together. Turn bag right side out and pin and stitch 1 of the strips of bias binding to base, right sides together, with a ⅜in (1cm) seam allowance, joining bias ends together with a straight seam.

10 Turn binding over to sides of bag, pin under a ⅜in (1cm) hem, and press. Stitch in a "ditch" from the base of the bag through to the sides, catching the binding on the sides of the bag.

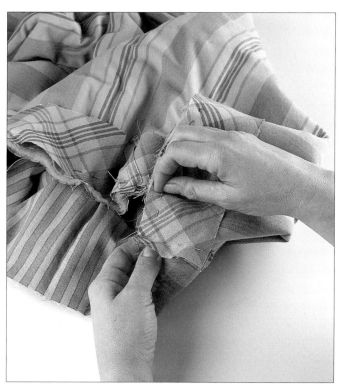

11 Pin and stitch other strip of bias binding to top of bag right sides together, with a ⅜in (1cm) seam allowance, joining bias ends together with a straight seam. Turn binding over to inside of bag, pin under hem, and press. Stitch in a "ditch" from the outside of the bag through to the inside, catching the binding all the way around on the inside as with the base in step 10.

12 Hammer eyelets in position at equal intervals around the bag top, following the instructions on the package. Here 8 eyelets were used, positioned at approximately 4in (10cm) intervals, all 5½in (14cm) from the bag top. Remember that you need an even number of eyelets so that when you lace the rope through, both ends will finish up on the outside.

Making the Tassels

1 To make string tassels, wind the knitting cotton 80 times around a piece of cardboard, 20in (50cm) wide.

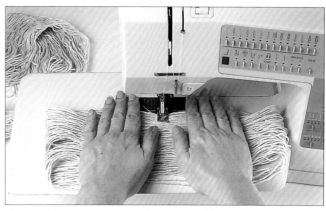

2 Carefully slide the string from around the piece of cardboard and stitch across the middle of the hank, using a long stitch setting. Cut the loops at either end as evenly as possible.

3 Hold the stitching line of the hank around the length of rope and stitch in position by hand with a darning needle. Wrap more string around to strengthen the join and stitch over and over until the tassel is secure.

4 Flip string over to cover rope end and wind more string tightly around the tassel. Stitch through it to hold firmly in place and trim the tassel. Thread the other end of the rope through the eyelets so that both ends are outside the bag. Trim the rope to the desired length and make and attach a second tassel following the steps above.

Variation

Blue Heraldic

This mythical beast, frolicking among stylized flowers on cerulean cotton, would look handsome lined with striped cotton in coffee and cream. The small blue check stands out crisply as the binding and base, and the tassels are in matching colors.

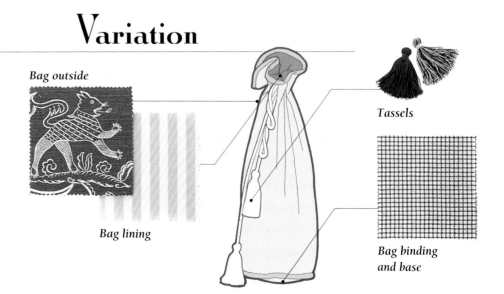

Bag outside

Bag lining

Tassels

Bag binding and base

Picnic Tablecloth and Bag

Civilized equipment to make your picnics stylish and comfortable: a summery tablecloth or blanket, and a bag to carry it and other picnic essentials.

SUMMER IS THE SEASON for relaxed enjoyment; it is the time for discovering grassy, tree-shaded banks by sun-dappled rivers; for enjoying a midnight feast under the stars, or iced drinks on hazy mornings among the sand dunes. But, as anyone knows who has thrown themselves into *al fresco* living, nothing dampens enthusiasm quite as effectively as a wet blanket and a dew-soaked posterior.

There is no need for these indignities. Waterproof fabrics have been transformed from the rigid, plastic-coated cottons familiar from many a sticky table, to an array of interesting and attractive alternatives – from brilliant man-made fibers to the sumptuous sheen of fine, rubber-backed silk. They are not expensive and, paired with a deliciously fruity print on tightly woven furnishing grade cotton, can serve as a tablecloth-cum-rug.

Cotton corduroy would be suitable for a heavier-duty rug. Whatever you choose, the tablecloth will only take an hour or so to make and will soon become indispensible. You can use it to cover garden tables and seats at home as well as on outings.

The other problem with open-air eating is carrying everything. While a plastic cool-bag may be an unfortunate necessity for salads and chilled drinks, this bag is perfect for stuffing with the tablecloth, a book, and even something to eat or drink, and simply slinging over your shoulder. Its long handles, securely stitched for added strength, have been specially designed with this in mind, and its pocket, large enough to hold a thermos, bottle, or cutlery, neatly solves the problem of what to do with all those awkward odds and ends essential for the perfect picnic.

MATERIALS

For a tablecloth 47in (120cm) × 59in (148cm)

Furnishing cotton for front: 1⅓yd (1.22m) of 60in (150cm) fabric
Rubberized silk for backing: 1⅓yd (1.22m) of 60in (150cm) fabric
Matching sewing thread
Tissue paper

For a bag 15in (38cm) wide × 18in (46cm) deep

Furnishing cotton for bag outside and pocket: ⅔yd (61cm) of 60in (150cm) fabric
Rubberized silk for lining: ½yd (46cm) of 60in (150cm) fabric
Herringbone webbing for handles: 4½yd (4m) of 1in (2.5cm) webbing
Matching sewing thread
Tissue paper

The Fabrics

A ripe collection of "summer fruit" colors in a rich furnishing cotton, backed with celadon green rubberized silk. The bag is lined with the silk and has strong natural herringbone webbing handles.

Tablecloth backing and bag lining

Tablecloth front and bag outside

Bag handles

COMPONENTS

*Below are the elements needed for a 47in (120cm) × 59in (148cm) tablecloth
and a 15in (38cm) × 18in (46cm) bag*

Bag outside: 2 pieces, each 16in (40.5cm) × 20in (50cm)

Tablecloth front: 47¾in (122cm) × 59¾in (150cm)

Tablecloth backing: 47¾in (122cm) × 59¾in (150cm)

Bag lining: 2 pieces, each 16in (40.5cm) × 20in (50cm)

Bag handles: 4½yd (4m)

Bag pocket: 7in (18cm) × 20in (51cm)

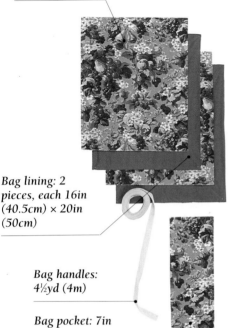

Making the Tablecloth

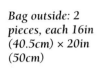
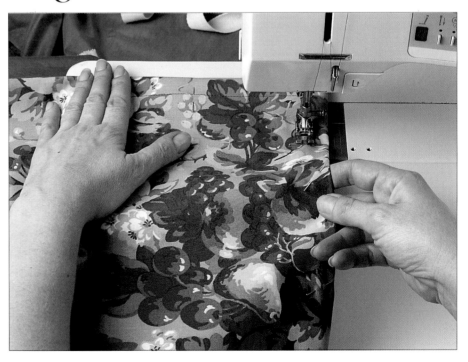

1 Mark and cut out front and backing following components photograph. Pin front and backing right sides together. Stitch along all 4 sides with a ⅜in (1cm) seam allowance, leaving a 12in (30cm) gap on one side to turn cloth right side out. If rubber sticks to the feed-plate of the machine, stitch through tissue paper.

2 Trim corners to reduce bulk and turn cloth right side out. Hand stitch the opening and overstitch the cloth using machine, 1in (2.5cm) from the edge, with thread to match underside.

Making the Bag

1 Mark and cut out fabric for bag following components photograph. Fold fabric for pocket in half, right sides together, and stitch across short side, with a ½in (1.25cm) seam allowance.

2 Turn pocket right side out and topstitch pocket across the top, 1in (2.5cm) from edge, with matching thread.

3 Pin pocket so it is centered on piece of fabric that will be bag front and stitch along bottom of pocket 1in (2.5cm) from edge with matching thread.

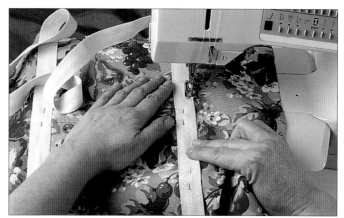

4 Cut 2 pieces of tape, each 79in (200cm) long, for handles. Using sides of pocket as your guide, pin tape from base of bag front to top, covering pocket sides. Stitch 1 side of tape in place, turning across tape 1in (2.5cm) from bag top to leave seam allowance for attaching lining. Stitch down other edge of tape and attach.

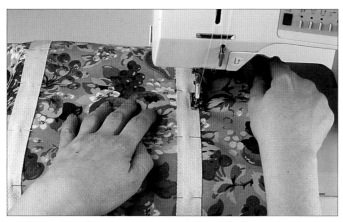

5 Pin and stitch in same way to attach handle loop to bag back, measuring to make sure handles are in the same position as on the front.

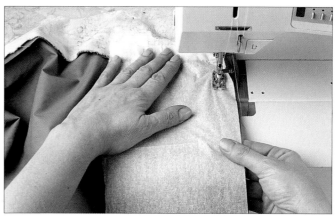

6 With right sides together, pin and sew bag front to lining piece at top with ½in (1.25cm) seam allowance, taking care not to catch handles. Attach second lining piece to bag back in same manner. Matching top seams, stitch bag and lining front and backs right sides together with ½in (1.25cm) seam allowance sewing through tissue paper if rubber sticks.

Making the bag (cont.)

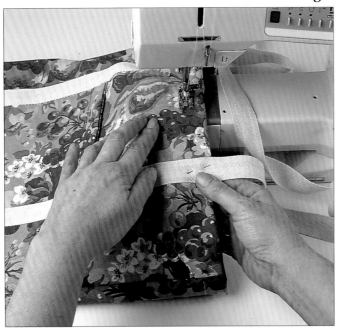

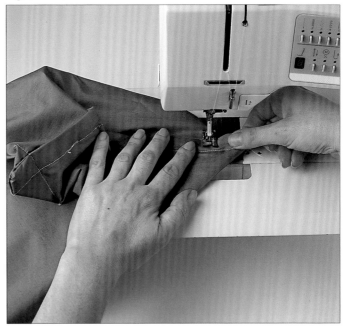

7 Press side seams open with a cool iron. Turn right side out and topstitch all around top opening and handles 1in (2.5cm) away from edge to neaten.

8 Create a French seam (see p. 12) by sewing a ¼in (6mm) seam across the base of the bag on the outside, taking in both fabric and lining. Turn bag inside out and sew a ½in (1.25cm) seam along inside of base. Sew across corners to give the bag a rectangular base and trim corner fabric. Turn right side out.

Variation

Reds and Greens

This mixture of solid, stripes, pattern, and checks are linked by their carefree summer garden colors and would combine well on cloth and picnic bag, with handles of bright red tape.

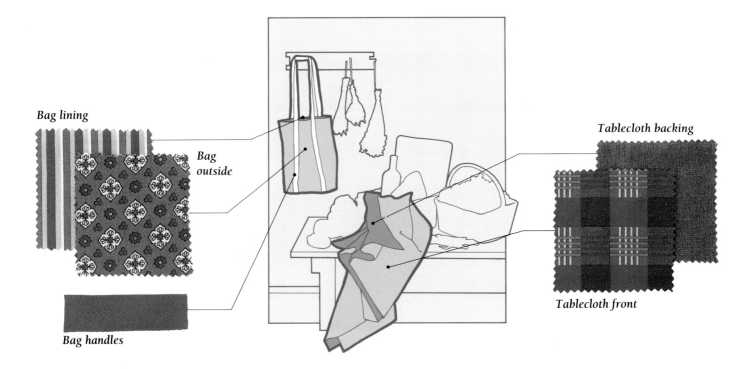

Bag lining

Bag outside

Tablecloth backing

Bag handles

Tablecloth front

Index

Acknowledgements

This book has been very much a team effort, and would not exist at all but for the nifty needlework of Doreen James, who had the task of making every project, and the generosity of Bogod's, who loaned us the Bernina 1230 with which she did so. The editor, Colin Ziegler, took on the role of indefatigable sheepdog with a demon eye for detail – the success of this book is almost entirely his achievement – and the designer, Steven Wooster, made much of what he had to work with. Our photographer, Clive Streeter, frequently Polaroided and bracketed far into the night, and Artemi Kyriacou, his assistant, smiled and labored until the last buttonhole had been stitched into submission. Lucinda Egerton, with the help of Ali Edney, performed the magical feat of putting the projects in a charming and convincing context. Textiles came from all sorts of places – Liberty of London have a glorious and surprising variety, The Textile King, Soho Silks and Borovick are unfailing sources of inspiration, and anyone who cannot make it to Delhi can well make do with the aptly named New Rainbow Textiles in Southall.

I would also like to thank the following who were kind enough to lend us materials featured in the book.

Antiques
Decorative Living, 55 New Kings Road, London SW6
Judy Greenwood, 657 Fulham Road, London SW6
Robert Young, 69 Battersea Bridge Road, London SW11

Curtain Poles
Artisan, 797 Wandsworth Road, London SW8

Fabrics
Celia Birtwell, 71 Westbourne Park Road, London W2
Laura Ashley Home Furnishings, 7–9 Harriet Street, London SW1
Mulberry (Fabrics and Furniture), Fourth Floor, Harvey Nicholls, Sloane Street, London SW1
Osborne and Little, 304 Kings Road, London SW3

Flooring
Afia Carpets, Chelsea Harbour Design Centre, Lots Road, London SW10
Crucial Trading (Coir Matting/Seagrass), 77 Westbourne Park Road, London W2
Fired Earth (Tiles), Middle Aston, Oxon

Furniture
Graham and Green (Furniture, Decorative Objects, and China), 4 & 7 Elgin Crescent, London W11
Liberty, 210/220 Regent Street, London W1
Somerset Country Furniture (Painted Furniture), 632 Fulham Road, London SW6
The Shaker Shop, 322 Kings Road, London SW3